**Captain Matthew Mitchell**

*Captain Matthew Mitchell*

**Frances Jewel Dickson**

*Frances Jewel Dickson*

# Skipper

## The Sea Yarns
## of
## Captain Matthew Mitchell

### by
### Frances Jewel Dickson

Pottersfield Press, Lawrencetown Beach, Nova Scotia, Canada

**Library and Archives Canada Cataloguing in Publication**

Dickson, Frances Jewel
    Skipper : the sea yarns of Captain Matthew Mitchell / Frances Jewel Dickson.

ISBN 978-1-897426-10-4

1. Mitchell, Matthew, 1917-.  2. Fisheries–North Atlantic Ocean–History.
3. Seafaring life–North Atlantic Ocean.  4. Ship captains–Nova Scotia–Biography.
5. Fishers–Nova Scotia–Biography.  6. Lunenburg (N.S.)–Biography.  I. Title.

SH20.M58D53 2009          639.2'2092          C2009-902698-8

**Cover design by Gail LeBlanc**

**Cover photo by Curtis Trent**

**Author photo by Robert Hirtle, Lighthouse Media Group**

Pottersfield Press acknowledges the financial support of the Government of Canada through the Book Publishing Industry Development Program for our publishing activities. We also acknowledge the ongoing support of the Canada Council for the Arts, which last year invested $20.1 million in writing and publishing throughout Canada. We also thank the Province of Nova Scotia for its support through the Department of Tourism, Culture and Heritage.

Pottersfield Press
83 Leslie Road
East Lawrencetown, Nova Scotia, Canada, B2Z 1P8
Website: www.pottersfieldpress.com
To order, phone toll-free 1-800-NIMBUS9 (1-800-646-2879)
Printed in Canada

Since this is the story of Matthew Mitchell's life, as the author, I wish to defer the dedication of this book to him.

## DEDICATION

*To my parents, Frederick and Violet, for putting the sea in my blood. In memory of my wife Olive, who steered the home ship alone while I was at sea. For all my fishing comrades and to everyone who made my years at the Fisheries Museum of the Atlantic so memorable.*
*— Matthew Mitchell*

# CONTENTS

## Foreword by Ralph D. Getson

It was my great privilege and honour to have recorded Matthew Mitchell's life stories as a deep-sea fisherman.

Our weekly sessions at the Fisheries Museum of the Atlantic were like a voyage back in time guided by a most capable pilot. Matthew told of his experiences from a young boy in the bow of a dory off Newfoundland, to master of a modern stern trawler out of Lunenburg, Nova Scotia. In his own quiet way without boasting or embellishing he shared many tales of his life at sea and on shore.

Matthew has the great gift of being able to tell a good story. Like a netmaker, he can effortlessly weave a yarn to catch you right in the moment. I first met Matthew in 1977 when I was a greenhorn guide at the Fisheries Museum and he was shore captain of the museum fleet. Matthew was a great source of information on many aspects of the fishery. He had firsthand knowledge of dory fishing on the Grand Banks. He was a doryman aboard *Pasadena II*, *Bessemer*, *Mahaska*, *Alcala II*, *Marjorie and Dorothy*, *Isabel F. Spindler* and the famous *Bluenose* during the latter days of the age of schooner fishing. He went on to take part in the early years of the "modern" fishery, fishing with huge nets from motorized trawlers. He had his first command as master of *Cape North*, one of the first of the successful fresh fish trawlers.

Matthew had a cod end full of his own sea stories but was also a great listener and gathered stories from earlier times told to him by retired captains and fishermen he befriended. He became the keeper of these wonderful stories that so poignantly illustrate the hardships of the fishery. As if it were a solemn obligation to those who had gone before, he strived to ensure the stories he related were told exactly as they had been told to him. A keeper of stories, he also willingly shared them with thousands of visitors to the Fisheries Museum for over thirty years. Many museum visitors have commented that the time spent talking with Captain Mitchell was for them "the highlight of their trip to Nova Scotia."

Here then, often in his own words, are Matthew Mitchell's memories of his life on the ocean wave. Another chapter in the great fishing heritage of Atlantic Canada.

# Author's Note

This book is based on a collection of stories recounted by Captain Matthew Mitchell to Ralph D. Getson, Curator of Education at the Fisheries Museum of the Atlantic, who recorded them verbatim some seven years ago. This chronicle of Matthew's life experiences was intended for family and friends and as a legacy for future Mitchell generations.

I was able to convince Captain Mitchell that his life-long association with the Atlantic fishery would be of interest to the general population. He agreed to let me join my voice to his in depicting the events that lured him from his rich and colourful Newfoundland heritage to Lunenburg, Nova Scotia, always at the whims of the sea.

It has been my privilege to cooperate with Captain Mitchell in the evolution of his memoirs into this book.

Now past his ninetieth year, he exudes a remarkable spirit and energy that inspire those fortunate enough to spend time in his company.

# Introduction

From the age of sailing vessels, ever since Europeans settled on its coastal shores, Newfoundland has been releasing her sons to the sea at a tender age. Boys as young as ten eagerly followed grandfathers, fathers, uncles and brothers on family boats to learn firsthand the craft that, more often than not, became their life's work. At sea and on shore, these young apprentices participated to the best of their abilities in the time-honoured methods of catching and processing fish while learning the skills and secrets of their forefathers' trade.

Matthew Mitchell was one of those boys. Born in 1917 in a small fishing village on the south coast of the Burin Peninsula, young Matt saw his future in the sea. After all, did Newfoundland not boast of the richest cod fishery in the world? In 1929, the forces of nature intervened when an earthquake, followed by three powerful tidal waves, struck forty-six coastal communities on the Burin Peninsula, including Matt's village of Port au Bras.

It was ironic that these now devastated communities, because they relied on fish as their currency, had not been as affected by the bank crash of 1929 as the rest of North America. Now the fish were gone and communities like the Mitchells' would face a decade of severe economic hardship. It would take the advent of World War II to bring options to these resilient Newfoundlanders.

Matthew Mitchell would not wait ten years for the fish to return to his shores. At the age of fifteen he got his first chance on a fishing schooner. He fell into a pattern of working on vessels that sailed out of Nova Scotia ports and by the mid-1930s he was calling Lunenburg home. It would be twenty years before he returned to his native village.

Matt fished mostly in two-man dories, night and day, braving the North Atlantic in all seasons and all kinds of weather, for very little pay. In 1947, when trawlers were gaining popularity as fishing boats, Matt went to work on the *Cape North*, one of the first trawlers to fish out of Lunenburg. He was taken on as a deckhand but would work his way through the ranks until he was offered command of the *Cape North* less than ten years later.

When Captain Mitchell retired from going to sea in 1977, the sea was not ready to let him go. He was approached by the Fisheries Museum in Lunenburg to serve as its shore captain. The museum was still under development and, in characteristic fashion, Captain Mitchell embraced the challenge with gusto, tackling whatever task was at hand, none being too menial, and never counting the hours. He would remain the Fisheries Museum shore captain for more than thirty years.

In this book of memoirs, from the perspective of his ninety-plus years, Captain Mitchell reflects back on his life experiences. From the rich enduring culture of his Newfoundland heritage, to a half century at sea from dories to trawlers, to captivating the interest of visitors to the Fisheries Museum from all over the world, Matthew Mitchell remains a genuine epitome of the era of "Wooden Ships and Iron Men."

# Chapter 1

# Offspring of

# Coastal Newfoundland

## Life in an Outport

Matthew Mitchell was born in Port au Bras, on the Burin Peninsula of Newfoundland, on June 12, 1917. Like most men in this village of some ninety families, his father Frederick and paternal grandfather Matthew were fishermen.

Fishing dominated the villagers' lives, and while not bringing them great wealth, it provided a wholesome living with plenty to eat and all the clothes they needed. Most families owned a jack boat (a four-sail, one-dory vessel measuring forty feet) or a schooner (a fore-and-aft-rigged ship with two or more masts, the forward mast being smaller that the others). Those who did not were otherwise equipped for fishing with traps and trawl gear dories or other types of small boat.

In the absence of roads leading outside the peninsula, boats not only provided a living from the sea but were also essential modes of transportation to other communities, such as Trinity Bay where Matthew's mother Violet Piercey hailed from. Realistically, though, such journeys by boat were seldom undertaken and Matthew can only recall meeting a couple of uncles on his mother's side of the family.

A dory under sail, full of the catch of the day, passes fishing schooners.

Late Grandfather Mitchell's house was home to young Matt and his family for the first couple of years of his life; subsequently, a new house was built next door.

It was a two-storey structure set on cement blocks, with a flat roof sloping to the back. The house had wood clapboard siding and, in typical Newfoundland fashion, was painted white. The downstairs consisted of three rooms: the kitchen, where a Victoria combination wood-coal stove presided; the dining room-parlour the locals referred to as "the good room"; and a large storage room, Violet's domain, which she used as a pantry. Three bedrooms made up the upstairs. The ceilings were hard pine and the floors were planked in wide, painted-over softwood boards; at times the floors would be covered with sail canvas as well that would also be coated with paint.

In keeping with houses of that era in that part of the world, there was no central heating or indoor plumbing. The kitchen stove and a smaller version of it in the parlour provided heat. Water was fetched in buckets from the dug well and the full buckets would be placed on a stand inside the porch. A galvanized tub served as clothes washer and bathtub. Violet carried out a major housecleaning spring and fall.

Port au Bras, circa 1925, on the Burin Peninsula of Newfoundland as Matt would have seen it in his childhood.

This section of Port au Bras could have been called Mitchell Row as Matt's house was flanked on either side by the dwellings of his uncles Sam and Joe.

Port au Bras had a one-room school that housed grades one to ten. A young female assistant teacher looked after the lower grades. A male teacher, who also acted as principal, taught the more senior classes and saw to it that standards and discipline were maintained. Matthew calls to mind that during Mr. King and Mr. Toope's tenures you could hear a pin drop.

When the Governor General of Newfoundland visited, he came by destroyer and a school holiday would be declared. Matthew recalls one such occasion when his mother had given him a nickel, which he saved to buy handmade ice cream. "Was the best tasting thing I ever had in my life was that ice cream," he says.

In the early 1900s, four religious denominations were predominant in Burin: Anglican, Catholic, Methodist, and the Salvation Army. The Mitchell family were practicing Anglicans.

"Oh gollies, we had a lovely church," says Matthew. "In fact, I believe the head carpenter was from up in the Annapolis Valley of Nova Scotia."

A small building housed the joint telegraph and postal services. In the case of the telegraph, news came over the wires from St. John's; the mail arrived by mail-boat or courier from Burin. Prior to the advent of radio, the small office kept villagers connected to the outside world. During World War I, the postmistress, Josie Churchill, would copy in her handwriting the news that came over the telegraph into a book. Then she would place the book, opened at the appropriate page, in a window where it could be viewed by the public. There was always someone prepared to oblige by reading the news out loud for the benefit of those who could not read. People gathered at the telegraph-post office to discuss current events. During wartime, news from the various theatres of war would be eagerly awaited.

After 1930, when radios became available, smaller gatherings were common at the homes of residents fortunate enough to own a battery-operated unit. It would be 1960 before the telephone reached the Burin Peninsula.

Despite the lack of modern technology, good times abounded in the region. There were concerts, dances and hot suppers. A number of organizations sponsored the dances: Orange Lodge, Masonic Lodge, Fishermen's Lodge, the Knights of Columbus and the Salvation Army. The supper menus ranged from soup such as beef barley or split pea, to full meals like corned beef and cabbage or roast beef topped with a large Yorkshire pudding.

For what needs could not be met at Cheeseman's or other small stores in Port au Bras, the fishermen went to Burin, some three miles away. Burin was the hub of the region with a lot of schooners on site and, prior to 1929, it was a going concern. "It was like a city," Matthew says. When the *Bluenose* ran ashore in Placentia, she was repaired on a Burin slip. A number of fish companies had their own retail store in the area: Lafever's in Bull's Cove, Sheaves' in Path End, Alfy Marshall's,

Bartlett's, Tom Hollett's, Bill Hollett's, Cody's, Inkman's, and Bishop's.

A ferry service was launched by the Newfoundland government in 1918. The motorized boat, some forty feet in length, featured a housing compartment capable of accommodating thirty to forty passengers. The ferry made two daily runs, leaving Burin at 9 a.m. and 1 p.m. Port au Bras was the last port of call. However, Port au Bras was dropped from the schedule after the first couple of years of operation, which was unfortunate considering the ferry had served to carry incoming and outgoing mail to and from the half-dozen ports between there and Burin.

One year when Matt was at St. Pierre with his father, the *Corticelli* ran ashore at Langlade Reach before reaching St. Pierre. Cousin Bill and Gabriel Brown, a distant relative, were aboard her and Matt went out when she was being towed into St. Pierre. He stayed aboard for a couple of weeks while the ship was being repaired and Matthew recalls, "I got to be a pretty big fellow running around with them guys there in St. Pierre, and I enjoyed every minute of it." He used to help the cook; being rum-runners, they had nothing but the best in food. Matt returned home with piles of clothing and other gifts from his time aboard the *Corticelli* while she was on the slip.

Matthew also recalls a steamer running ashore at Cat Island. Some of the villagers were out wrecking her, taking whatever they could salvage. Two fellows from his village made a return trip to the grounded ship to retrieve something that had caught their eye earlier. Tragically, while they were aboard, the ship slid off the rock and both men were lost.

Another local man, Jim Butler, was lost at sea while serving on the *Mary Hirtle*. This occurred before the tidal waves of 1929 and Matthew reminisces, "We had a swamp-bottom boat. The three brothers of us, we were out cutting kelp to use on the land for manure. We looked and we seen the minister coming on the other side of the harbour. We knew that when you seen a minister coming there was something going on. This is where he went in to Mrs. Butler's. Jim got washed overboard. He was to the pump and she shipped a sea and he got knocked overboard."

The August gales of 1926-27 that heaped devastation on vessels and lives from Lunenburg, Nova Scotia, also affected the Burin Peninsula. Matthew can remember seeing the schooners in his village all ashore, and a flurry of activity around them, while the people tried to hold them fast.

One fall a skipper was taking his schooner to St. John's with a load of fish. His wife was aboard and his brothers were crew. As they laid calm off Cape Race, an ocean liner ran through the schooner. It was at night and the skipper was in his bunk down below when he heard a noise. He went up on deck only to witness his boat sinking quickly; there was no sign of anyone else aboard. He grabbed onto a nearby dory thwart and held on. It was a clear night and rumour had it there was a party going on aboard the liner. A passenger on the wing deck spotted the man clinging to the dory thwart and alerted an officer, who took quick action. The captain of the schooner was saved but his family drowned.

Grandfather Mitchell's schooner was lost when his mate took her out and was never heard from again. On that November anniversary, at dusk in the harbour at Port au Bras, the lost schooner would appear. When he was a small boy, Matt's mother would take him by the hand saying, "Oh my gollies, we've got to hurry up and go up on the hill to see your grandfather's boat coming in."

Matthew remembers, "You could see the shadow like a schooner coming in, all the sails on her. When he come in you could hear him lowering the sails, the jib and jumbo, the blocks and everything creaking. You could hear the chain when they dumped the anchor overboard. She would come up head to it and take down the rest, then take the mainsail down. After everything was done, it just disappeared." The yearly apparition was a favourite spectacle in the village.

One of the few fires in his home port stands out in Matthew's mind. His Aunt Bertha was married to a man named John Sam and their house burned down. The house was near the school, and the day of the fire the schoolchildren, while out playing, observed John digging by one of the cement blocks that had served as support for the house. Uncle John hauled up a rubber hip boot, and in front of the mesmerized children, spilled a pile of gold nuggets from the boot onto the ground.

Some fishing captains from Newfoundland set their sights on foreign ports such as Portugal, Spain, France and the Caribbean. They would export fish and return with cargos of molasses, salt and other goods. Some of the foreign-going skippers from Port au Bras were Ambrose Bennett, George Bennett and Charlie Clark. "Oh yes, my heavens," says Matthew, "them guys cut their eye teeth on the Western Ocean. They all had big schooners."

Captain Charlie Clark was once asked by Murray's ship company in St. John's to take a loaded vessel to Marseilles, France. The fellow from Murray's asked Charlie, "Do you think you can take her there?" Skipper Clark answered, "Does the sun shine there?" "Yes," the old fellow replied. Then the skipper asked, "Is there any water there?" Again the answer was yes. Seeing that the proposed voyage met his basic requirements, Captain Clark declared, "By gee, I can take her there!"

There was a fall ritual the fishermen of Port au Bras engaged in. There was not much wood around the village. "It was pretty barreny," Matthew recalls. "You'd get some small wood, but we used to always use our boat to go down around Marystown or Cape Roger and those places where there was good wood. My father and uncles would bring a load apiece up. That made three loads; that was a year's wood everybody had."

One November Matt and his cousin Bill asked permission to take the family boat and go down for a load of wood. After some coaxing, the senior Mitchells consented and the boys were on their way in, as Matt calls it, a good breeze of wind. Bill was a daring sort of a fellow and before long, the boat was "hove out" on her beam end. They had the ballast loose down in her so it shifted while they were on Jean de Baie Bight, where the weather could get quite dirty. They drifted into

Parker's Cove where they dumped the anchor overboard. "She was hatch coamings in the water you," says Matthew, "and we had the dory astern, towing the dory. That old thing could have sank anytime you."

Some of the men in Parker's Cove noticed the vessel turned over on its side rail and came aboard to help the boys pump her out and set her upright. They finally made it to Cape Roger some three miles away where they knew there was a great forest of birch and whitings. The whitings or white-ends, dead spruce trees stripped of their bark, were useful for fish-flake platforms and also made excellent firewood.

The cousins cut wood until they figured they had a load. The next step was to dump their harvest into the Cape Roger River. They had been careful to first string pieces of wood tied together at an appropriate spot in the river to stop the wood from going adrift. It was November and Matthew remembers, "The name of God, what we went through out there in that cold water clearing that up" because some of the wood got caught up on the rocks. They managed to get the boat loaded below and on deck, being careful not to make it top-heavy.

They left Cape Roger and in retrospect Matthew says, "If we had come on I think we'd have made it the finest kind, but it was getting pretty dirty and we decided we would go into Rushoon. We went into Rushoon and I'll tell you what saved us in there was a fellow by the name of Bill Cheeseman. We had the two anchors out to her and she went adrift and he seen it and he come. They had lots of rope, you know, because they had all kinds of trap gear lines and everything. He tied it to his wharf and come out and brought the end out and put it around our chain. We were all set then."

They laid there until the storm passed and when a little draft of wind from the north came they decided to go. It was smooth sailing home in spite of having to cross Jean de Baie Bight again. Once safely home the cousins could boast of a great load of whitings and birch.

One June when Matt turned thirteen years old, he went with his father and cousin Bill to Trepassey, Cape St. Mary's and Cape Pine to fish. One calm, foggy, rainy morning they anchored down at a place called Mistaken Point. The cousins had under-run (re-baited) their trawl in the dory and returned to the vessel to find the quarters full of fish Matt's father had jigged aboard and himself toppled over on top of the fish. The boys could not tell what was wrong with him but managed to get him down to his bunk. They then busied themselves getting the boat underway to go into Trepassey for help. Once there Matt went ashore in search of oranges to feed his father, who could not manage to eat anything else.

The lady who ran the store told the concerned boy that the only person likely to have oranges would be the village priest. Undeterred, Matt went up to Father Wilson's house and told the woman caretaker who answered the door that he needed to see the priest. This man of the cloth cut a formidable figure with his colossal frame draped in a dark robe, but Matt managed to overcome his nervousness and told the priest his story. After listening intently Father Wilson declared, "Your father doesn't need oranges, he needs a doctor." He offered to go aboard with the boy and gathered up some fruit before leaving the house.

Having assessed the man in the bunk, the priest turned to the boys and said, "Your father is dying of double pneumonia. We have to get him to St. John's." Then he said he would arrange for someone to come for him that night. Although the diagnosis had shocked and frightened Matt, he was still mindful of the slowness of transportation in those days and of poor road conditions. His young instincts told him these things made a trip to St. John's too risky and that the water route was their best option even if it meant sailing some seventy miles. So he mustered all his courage and informed Father Wilson that he and Bill would be taking his father home by boat.

That night, Matthew recalls, "She breezed up and she got dirty and I was running this thing, steering it, and Bill was out trying to get the jib in, out on the bowsprit. When she used to run off, she used to run right level with him out on that bowsprit."

When they figured they were close to home, they stopped the boat. In fact, they actually did not know where they were, the visibility was so bad. Looking back Matthew says, "Look here, as the Lord should have it, when it cleared up we were only about a mile. If we would have went further we'd have been up on a rock."

Once they got the sick man ashore, they fetched Dr. Moseley from Burin. Doc confirmed Father Wilson's diagnosis. Matthew recollects his father had quite a siege of double pneumonia. In the absence of hospitals, he was cared for at home where the doctor visited him every day. Matthew credits old Dr. Moseley with "pulling him out of it." Unfortunately, once cured of pneumonia, Frederick Mitchell, who was in his forties at the time, was left unable to walk for a couple of years. However, he lived into his eighties and remained healthy until the last couple of years of his life.

On a happier note, when the big schooners were in Burin, Matt and his friends would go up there and go aboard. The *Carrie and Nellie* was one of those schooners, and Matt had many a meal aboard her. Matthew remembers a particularly pleasant stay aboard the *C.A. Anderson* from Lunenburg when Captain Daniel Mosher had her. Frederick Mitchell had been hired by the captain to haul bait for them and Matt had tormented his father to go along. He was successful and stayed aboard that vessel for one whole memorable week.

## Nuts and Bolts of the Inshore Fishery

Matt gained early exposure to the inshore fishery by going out to the trap skiffs with his father and uncles. Trap season was usually June to August. The cod traps were fabricated from knitted twine in the shape of a square some twelve to fifteen fathoms (seventy-two to ninety feet) square. A leader, also made of twine and measuring some sixty to one hundred fathoms (360 to 600 feet) in length, was connected to the trap door and would either be anchored or attached to the land. These contrivances were effective in leading many fish into the traps from which they could not escape.

Two children on the flakes, surveying their domain of fish.

The children would help load the boat until it was full then put the rest of the fish in cod bags that would be towed in. Once they reached their stage, a covered platform made of rough wood projecting over the water and supported by large sticks called shores, the fish would be flung one by one from the boat to the stage using a one-prong fork called a pew. The children were eager to assist at every stage of the process and this was truly a hands-on learning experience.

Matthew recalls, "Us kids used to get a great kick out of helping to fork them up on the stage head, and then of course we were right into it helping to gut them and clean them when they were splitting them and getting them ready to salt."

There were three initial steps in getting the fish ready to salt. First, a throater would cut the fish's throat and slit the fish open, then a second man, the header, would break the head off and remove the innards; the third man, the splitter, removed the sound bone or backbone. The fish was then washed and put in the hold until they were ready to spread and salt them. Twelve to fifteen days after the salting, the fish were washed again and placed on flakes, platforms built from vertical and horizontal poles called lungers or longers which would be

A fisherman in front of his store surrounded by a sea of drying cod.

spread with spruce boughs that would allow the air to circulate around the fish.

Toward the end of the day, when dampness began to permeate the air, the fish would be stacked in increasingly towering piles called faggots, a step taken to prevent moisture from penetrating the fish and slowing the drying process. The fish turned whiter as they dried. Once dry, the cod would be placed in the fishermen's own stores, in the storehouses of merchants, or even shipped in schooners destined for ports all over the world. The same processing steps applied to fish caught by fishermen using small boats propelled by oars or sails, which would be used to fish ten to fifteen miles off the coast.

Matt's family had a jack boat. Young Matt delighted in joining his father in the dory to go jigging for cod when the fish abounded. They would also fish for cod using baitless gear held afloat with bobbins. While waiting for the fish to bite, they would use hand lines weighted by a fish-shaped piece of lead with two hooks they would bait with herring or squid. "Look here," says Matthew, "you could feel them biting on behind you." In the fall this method of fishing would produce some nice cod to put in stores for the winter.

Most summers fishing was good around Burin. However, Matthew can recall one summer when, instead, cod was striking around the Gulf of St. Lawrence at a place called Sauker Cove. His folks followed the fish and brought home enough cod to pile the stores, as Matthew says, "right full of salt cod in one season. We were lucky, we had a good life. I had great parents and good neighbours."

## Fishing on the Grand Banks

The Bank or offshore fishery was conducted differently, although the method of processing the fish catches was the same. Schooners carrying four to twelve small dory boats fastened down in cradles on deck, were used to fish on the Banks. The size of the crew on a schooner varied depending on the number of dories, although a large crew would consist of twenty-eight men.

Once they reached the fishing grounds, the fishermen set out trawls, long lines anchored at both ends that were held up by buoys. Short lines with baited hooks were attached to the long lines. After a few hours had passed, the crew boarded the dories to check the trawls and remove the fish from the hooks. The catch was returned to the schooner, and when the vessel had a full trip of fish, they would be cleaned and salted on board. Several days later the crew would return to port to land the catch and pick up more bait.

When he was just fourteen years old, Matt got the chance to make his first trip to the Banks. His first cousin, Earl Mitchell, was skipper of the *Fish Hawk*, a handsome green four-dory vessel with a mainsail. The boat, built in Newfoundland and owned by Murray's ship company in St. John's, fished out of Little Bay. Now Matt had his chance to go out and was paired in the dory with Ernest Bennett, an experienced man. They headed for St. Pierre Bank and set their trawl out during the night.

It's a small boat in a large ocean and it wasn't always a calm day, as it was for this two-man crew with their trawl tub in the centre of the dory. Once they left the schooner, they were on their own until the skipper returned hours later. Sometimes dorymen went "astray" – meaning the captain couldn't find them. And sometimes they stayed astray.

The next morning, Matthew says, "It was thick of fog and no wind much. We left to go down for our outside buoy and missed it. That was my first day on the Banks in a dory and we got astray. We were astray for quite a few hours. Then we got aboard a vessel and it was Ab Joyce was captain and he was in a big new schooner at the time. I have got the name forgot right at the time being. I only come to know a lot of the men afterwards. All them fellows were a big hardy gang of men he had aboard and they were dressing fish.

"So anyway we got something to eat and Skipper Ab told us where our vessel was, so we left, which we shouldn't have done. We left and went and missed her again, just couldn't find her. Anyway in the afternoon, there was no wind much but

This three-masted schooner on the LaHave River, is on its way either to or from the fishing banks.

it was still thick of fog – it was an old foggy, rainy day. We anchored, which was the best thing we ever done.

"By then I was getting pretty sick because I was homesick, like any young lad would be. I was half seasick and every other bloody thing. Then I thought I heard something and I told my dorymate, who said, 'We'll haul up the anchor.' We did and all of a sudden, she rounded right up alongside of us!

"It was the *Iris and Verna* with Captain Bob Moulton. We got aboard. There was no wind see, and what I heard was the sails slatting. So anyway, we got aboard of him and of course we got down below. I knew Ern, Ern Moulton – afterwards he was married to my first cousin. In fact, we knew different fellows aboard there. Bob wouldn't let us go no more. He said he would put us aboard, if we got some wind, since he knew where our vessel was. Sure enough during the night we got up where our vessel was and he put us aboard. That is the only time in all my career that ever I was astray. I never ever was astray after that."

Captains habitually hired a boy as young as twelve to do odd jobs around the boat. This boy was referred to as the flunky. In foggy weather it was the flunky's job to blow the horn. The single horn had been replaced by a double patent horn made by the Power's company. It would be blown continually, supplemented by an occasional ringing of the bell.

Matthew explains, "If a dory went astray, there was a swivel, a small cannon on board. Someone would load that with powder and anything all, whatever they could get into it, they would fill the thing right full. The loaded swivel was then hoisted up on the jumbo halliard and tied there in such a way that it could be shifted whichever way you wanted the sound to go.

"What you would do, you had a wadding for a stopper into it and you also had one on a pole. You would light the one on the pole so that you'd be quite a ways from it and you would light that. Then you would run back of the dories there somewheres until it went off. That sound used to carry a long way. You would keep doing that until the dory would show up, unless you thought she wasn't going to come. That was mostly in the salt fishing days when you would be anchored, you'd be doing that."

There was an order to bringing the dories aboard. If you were under sail fishing, you generally used to lay to your "lee" (downwind) dory. The dories were numbered and the skipper would have them all in rotation; he knew how far to go for a dory and where she was lost. He would go back and forth over where the trawl was. Sometimes he would find the dories, sometimes not.

Matthew knew of a fellow who went astray every day. Although he would not be lost altogether, he was always an hour or two later than the next to last dory. One day his skipper swore to him, "I'm going to get a barrel of salmon net twine and give you the end of it so we don't have to be steaming all over the goddamned ocean looking for you!"

There are many yarns from home that come back to Matthew from time to time. One they used to hear out of Belleoram was about Captain John Marshall Fudge, who used to take an American vessel down to Newfoundland in the fall. It was said that he had the equivalent of a shop aboard.

He would stock up in the United States and when he was in Belleoram, his crew could get their oil clothes and anything else they needed right from the vessel.

Another yarn that circulated was about the *Marion Belle Wolfe* when Captain Ned Clarke had her. One time going to Newfoundland, he "hove her out" on her beam end. Apparently, some cargo they had picked up in Sydney had shifted. Word had it they steamed all night and played cards until the water came up to the floor and still they kept playing.

Matthew marvels, "Them fellas were tough. That didn't bother them."

## AN EARTHQUAKE AND TIDAL WAVES HIT HOME

The first twelve years of Matt's life evolved smoothly until one November day in 1929 that would turn his life upside down and change the lives of everybody he knew.

November 18 dawned a beautiful clear day in Port au Bras. A group of men were making repairs to the lighthouse on Iron Island, about a mile from the mouth of the harbour, where Matt's uncle Joe was the lightkeeper at the time. The workers on the island had completed their task and were rowing in while Matt and some other children were walking home from school. Suddenly, the ground started to shake. No one who felt it could tell what it was and some folks were even climbing up on their roofs thinking their chimney might be on fire. Some of the children turned back from home and headed down to the harbour where the men were coming in from Iron Island. Being dory and generally boat crazy, the village children were always eager to help unload gear, which they did that day, then went back home for supper.

An elderly man from St. Mary's had come up from the harbour to Uncle Joe's house. In those days, whoever came into the harbour was guaranteed their evening meal at someone or other's house and a place to stay overnight. A few other men had gathered at Joe's house and Matthew recalls, "I'll never forget that the old man was telling a yarn about some school children, that they had to go across a pond to school. One or more fell in and got drowned and it was right interesting to us kids to hear him telling the story." Later they would learn that three children had lost their lives in spite of the valiant efforts of their teacher to save them.

While the men were conversing, Aunt Pearl dropped her knitting and went outdoors. Then she came back in and without a word sat down and resumed knitting. Before long she was on her feet and out the door again. This time when she came back in, she said, "You guys best come out because there's something happening. All the boats are laid over on their beam ends in the harbour." It was dark by then and the men started heading for the beach where the Mitchells had their stores, when a roaring noise stopped them in their tracks. A wall of water was rolling in from a raging sea.

"It was legs do your duty then," Matthew reflects, as everyone turned on their heels and ran for higher ground. The first wave came in and cleaned the harbour right out. Two more tidal waves followed. A number of families, including the Mitchells, had their stores on a neck of beach about a hundred feet wide. Following the passage of the waves, the beach had been replaced by a channel wide and deep enough for a schooner to sail in and out.

Some of the heroic deeds that took place that night are recorded in *The History of Burin By Its Senior Citizens* in 1977. "The Telegraph Operator and Post Mistress of Port au Bras at the time, Miss Josephine Churchill, remained in her office until the water swirled around her feet. She had an open line with other offices in Burin and reported her concern to Miss Helen Dancey, operator at Great Burin, and that she would return to the office at 11 p.m. when the waters subsided. In the darkness, people climbed floating buildings in search of survivors. Men, forcing their way through doors and windows of half-submerged houses, and then swimming and leaping to safety with women and children in their arms, were common sights.

"Next morning, relief parties saw quantities of food, stored for the winter, washed up on the beaches. Furniture, houses, hay from cattle barns, fishing equipment, lines of

Monday's newly-washed clothes drifted with the tide. In places, waves rose 50 to 60 feet and swept everything before it when it receded."

In all, seven Port au Bras residents lost their lives in the tsunami. Matt's family was not spared. His aunt Frances, whose husband was away on a wood trip, wanted to attend an event at the school with her daughter Dorothy. She asked Marion, her eldest, to look after her baby brother while they were gone. Marion asked permission to take the baby next door for a visit and the four left the house together. At the gate, Aunt Frances realized she had forgotten her purse and told Marion, "You go ahead and we will go back to get my purse." While mother and daughter were in the house, the water came in. Although it was not a big wave like the ones in the harbour, it came in fast and floated the house off. "That was it," Matthew says somberly.

The coast guard cutter caught up with the house a couple of miles out to sea and went inside. The only sign of life was the cat they retrieved from a bed upstairs. The beds were all made and the upstairs rooms appeared as they would have before the house was pulled out to sea. Matthew supposes, "Those bodies had to have been down below." Matt fetched the cat from aboard the cutter and took it home.

William Henry Clarke's house was towed in by the cutter, then tied to the *Marion Belle Wolfe* for the winter and towed back to the village in the spring. Matthew remembers helping pull it up on land and settle it back on its foundation.

Some victims of the waves managed to escape tragedy. The Brushett family lived next door to Aunt Frances. Their house was also taken by the high tide, but the next tides returned it. The mother broke a window, from which she threw her five children out and jumped herself. All were saved.

Three brothers from Port au Bras were saved in Marshall's Dock when a boat they were in grounded between sunken wharves.

Every schooner in Matt's home harbour was sunk except for the *Bellaventure*. Matthew recalls, "Captain Henry Dibbin had her out in the harbour and I believe she was anchored right in the same place afterwards. She was the one that went in and out of the harbour with the water. In fact, he just came in – he brought her up from Marystown. He was supposed to take her to Burin the next day and anyway he did because she survived it."

Stories of damage in neighbouring outports were only trickling in as communication networks had been destroyed or badly damaged. One episode that sticks in Matthew's mind is what happened to Bartlett's general store in Burin, some three miles from his home. G.A. Bartlett was a fine, large store. The wave floated it off its foundation, turning it one hundred and eighty degrees, until a large rock stopped its motion. Miraculously, even fragile articles were not disturbed. The front door now opened toward the hill and Matthew recalls, "Customers could still go in for purchases until a new store was built."

Matthew summarizes the day after the disastrous tidal waves this way: "To add fat to the fire, the next day we got a breeze of wind and the weather turned dirty. The harbour was full of wreckage and with the snow and rain and everything, if ever you wanted to see a desolate-looking place that was it!"

Matt's family was fortunate that they did not lose their house. However, they lost their winter supply of food and coal, as well as their means to make a living: their boats, and fishing gear. Not that there were any fish left around the shore – the tidal wave had torn everything up.

Matthew reminisces, "For the next few years we didn't go anywheres because you had nothing to do nothing with and in fact, there was nothing until the war broke out. It was about ten years that this was going on." When World War II began, men were being called up to serve. The Americans built a base at Argentia which also provided jobs. When the fish started to return to the shores and a cold storage facility started up in Burin, the employment situation was looking up.

As a result of the tidal wave disaster, hundreds were left homeless and destitute, with no way to make a living. The government of Newfoundland brought in a compensation package. It was modest compared to the estimated $2 million of losses.

The program was based on targeting compensation to qualified goods and assets listed by the claimants. In all, the community of Port au Bras would receive some $38,000 of compensation.

For Matt's family, this represented some $1,100 which was to be shared with his uncle Samuel's family, as his father and uncle jointly owned their fishing equipment. In addition, Matt's father received $50 for loss of personal property. Claims for barrels of flour, molasses and winter provisions of salted fish were denied.

The South Coast Disaster Committee had given broad discretionary powers to a magistrate in Burin as to the allocation of monetary compensation and the distribution of food, lumber and clothing. This was a monumental task complicated by the fact that all the wharves in the outports had been destroyed. Matthew recalls that Cheeseman's store in his village was the distribution centre for clothes that had been donated by other countries.

Matthew tells the following yarn that was circulating at the time: "This fellow, he was a crippled man and he had no money for tobacco and so he used to smoke the loose tea leaves. Some nosy person told the magistrate that he was smoking his tea. The magistrate replied that if the man enjoyed smoking it better than drinking it then that was okay with him."

The government also brought in welfare – referred to as "the dole" – which was administered by the same magistrate from Burin. Each family's "dole order" amounted to only a couple of dollars and had to be stretched to meet their needs over a month.

Working fishing schooners at the mouth of the LaHave River.

A schooner makes its way into Ritcey's Cove, now known as Riverport, Nova Scotia.

Ritcey's Cove in the 1890s.

# Chapter 2

# Leaving Home to Go to Sea

## On-the-Job Training: The Silver Arrow

Early in the new year when Matt was fifteen, he happened to be around Burin when he noticed the *Silver Arrow* had come in. She was an eight-dory schooner and he really wanted a chance on a big vessel like that one. He also knew he was not yet capable of taking a dory himself and that there were a lot of unemployed people around the Peninsula at that time, seeing as the Depression was on. Matt knew that Joe Clark from back home was looking for work on a vessel. He thought he should inform Joe the *Silver Arrow* was in port and needed a crew, so he walked the three miles to his home. Joe promised he would get a place for Matt if he got a chance himself, so they went into Burin together and were both taken on.

They left Burin on January 10. The next day, they fished all day on St. Pierre Bank, hauling sixty to seventy lines of trawl and making two sets, at least six or seven tubs.

"Being just a young fellow I was all broke up at the end of the day," Matthew remembers. "That night it came a storm and we were running across the Gulf and I was seasick and home-sick. If ever I could have got off that thing I would never have gone out around the Head again. We got over to Louisbourg and it was just so bad there, if I would have knew the way home or had any money I'd have left then, but I couldn't get out of it. We were there until the weather straightened up a bit and came out fishing here to the westward. We got out and there wasn't no wind much but it was thick of snow."

Once they had the dories out and started hauling the trawl, Matt got a hook stuck in his hand. It hooked on just the same as it would hook onto a piece of bait. His dorymate filed the top of it off and "backed it back" but Matt still had to keep hauling the trawl in that predicament. When they got aboard that evening, they learned that a couple of dories had gone astray. The captain said, "They might be running for land" so they went looking for them. It was snowing with a little breeze of wind and they found the dories just as it was getting dark.

It was not long before Matt's hand started to swell. The captain decided to land him in Lunenburg, where there was a marine hospital. Matt had yet to be acquainted with Lunenburg. They arrived around one o'clock in the morning at Smith and Company's wharf, now the site of the Fisheries Museum and *Bluenose II* dock. Matt was put in hospital and the *Silver Arrow* went out again.

After Matt had been in hospital a few days, one morning Dr. Creighton, the attending physician, said to him, "You're okay, you can leave. Get ready and when I go, I'll take you into town." Matt asked, "Where am I going?" Doc rejoined, "What do you mean?" So Matt told him his story.

Dr. Creighton then asked, "What company are you?" Matt answered, "I don't know. I was just put in the hospital here and I don't know anything about Lunenburg and I don't know anyone in Lunenburg."

The doctor persisted, "Which vessel were you off?" That much Matt knew. Dr. Creighton took him to his office and told him, "You just sit here until I see my patients and I'll see what I can do."

When the doctor returned he had found out that the *Silver Arrow* fished out of Robin, Jones & Whitman's in Lunenburg and the name of the captain they needed to contact to arrange for Matt to be returned to his ship. When they dropped in on the skipper in question he seemed none too pleased to see them. When Dr. Creighton saw he was getting nowhere with his arguments, he told the captain, "Okay, you have a couple of hours to think about it, because this man is in the country illegally and when I go back I'm going to the Customs House and Immigration." This being 1933, Newfoundland was not yet a part of Canada.

This seemed to get the skipper's attention, for all of a sudden he was volunteering the information the doctor and his patient were after. He told them which day the vessel was going to be in Liverpool and gave Matt enough money to go up there and stay while he waited for the ship to come in; this amounted to a couple of dollars a night to cover lodging and breakfast plus train fare.

Dr. Creighton took Matt to the train station and described how to get to the Riverside Inn once he got to Liverpool, as the train would be pulling in after dark. He said he would call ahead and tell the folks at the inn to expect young Matt.

Matt was conscious he only had enough money to stay a couple of nights and that after breakfast, he would have nothing to eat for the rest of the day. The first thing he did after breakfast on the first morning was to go down to the docks to see where his vessel would be landing. He had no choice but to leave the inn on the second morning, so he ate his breakfast and headed out along the river on foot, carrying his small bundle of belongings. Then Matt recalls, "I saw the spars. That was one of the happiest moments of my life."

They fished in the area all winter. There was not much money to be made there as it was right in the Depression and fish were worth next to nothing.

In the spring they heard there was a lot of haddock around Ingonish in Cape Breton and that there was a demand for fresh herring. The *Silver Arrow* was chartered by Leonard's in Sydney to bring herring from Newfoundland and the Magdalen Islands. At the time, the entire crew aboard the *Silver Arrow* were from Newfoundland, so they would all be brought back where they came from. By all rights young Matt would also have to go, but Joe Clark, who was mate on the ship, said, "If he goes, I go!" So Matt and another fellow from down home were kept on and the rest of the crew was landed in Grand Bank. While in Newfoundland, the *Silver Arrow* acquired more than enough herring at twenty cents a barrel to fill the cold storage to capacity. The overflow was sold to lobster fishermen for two dollars a barrel.

On the last herring trip to Newfoundland Matt made on the *Silver Arrow*, he and some other crew came across a dance in a Harbour Breton hall around one o'clock in the morning. As fate would have it, the groom was Mr. King, principal at Port au Bras during Matt's last school year.

Meanwhile, back on the vessel, the captain was negotiating with two men who claimed they would guarantee having the ship loaded with herring at eighteen cents a barrel by the time the Customs House opened at 9 a.m. This was a more attractive offer than the one he had accepted earlier from another man offering to load the vessel with herring at twenty cents a barrel so the captain closed the deal with the two men. The pair made good their promise and the vessel was loaded and on its way to the Customs House before opening time.

Since they were too early for Customs, the vessel tied up to a nearby wharf and everyone except the engineer went ashore to walk around while they waited. Ironically, the wharf belonged to the man who had made the twenty cents a barrel offer. When he spotted the *Silver Arrow* tied to his dock, he and some of his buddies unfastened the lines. When the engineer saw what was happening he went down and, as Matthew recounts, "Gave her a kick ahead and she run in and got alongside further on the dock. I think him and the skipper had a pretty good set to about it." They made a couple of more trips to the Magdalen Islands for herring before the haddock struck.

The *Silver Arrow* with Captain Erlin Richards was then chartered by the day to carry haddock to Sydney. Matthew says Captain Richards was a great skipper, and was especially good with "young fellas" such as himself. The transport of haddock from Ingonish to Sydney went on for a couple of weeks. The only opportunity to sleep was during the daily run to and from

Ingonish, about two and a half hours, and that is if you were not pulling watch duty. After that, they followed the haddock up to L'Ardoise and got one decent load. Then the fish took off again and after a couple of meagre catches, it was time to go salmon "coasting."

When a vessel goes coasting, the fish is collected from a salmon merchant and delivered to the fish company that chartered the vessel – in this case, Leonard's in Sydney. The *Silver Arrow* headed for Labrador. When they returned to Sydney with a load of salmon, they learned that someone at Leonard's had decided to send a larger vessel to collect the salmon on the next trip. The plan called for the *Silver Arrow* to rendezvous with the larger vessel once the fish had been collected, take on the load and head back to Sydney. The theory was that the *Silver Arrow* could make better time than the larger vessel.

This may have been a good idea in principle, but in practice things did not go smoothly. The *Silver Arrow* was in and out of ports and up and down the coast a number of times before it could locate the larger vessel. The day they finally connected, there was quite a swell at sea and the bigger ship had two anchors out. Its captain insisted Captain Richards put out his anchor alongside and the three anchors became tangled. When Captain Richards returned to Sydney he made it quite clear to Leonard's he was not prepared to repeat such a frustrating, counter-productive trip. So the *Silver Arrow* was back on its own.

On another trip to Labrador, they ran short of ice. Matt and a couple of his crewmates went out to some small icebergs they called growlers to chop pieces of ice. The sea was rolling and Matt was sitting on an iceberg holding the dory alongside with both hands while the fellows in the dory chipped ice. Suddenly the growler rolled and Matt was dunked into the icy water. He was overboard long enough to get thoroughly chilled.

Fortunately, two vacationing nurses happened to be on board the vessel. They looked after Matt so he recovered quickly. One of the nurses was the daughter of Arthur Earle, a man from Carbonear who had been selling salmon to Captain

Richards. When the *Silver Arrow* stopped in Salmon Bight where the two nurses had been vacationing at Mr. Earle's camp, they had asked permission to sail up the coast on the schooner.

By that time the salmon was getting scarce. Rumour had it there was plenty of salmon in a more remote, less familiar harbour. Although Arthur Earle refused to go there, Captain Richards was keen so the *Silver Arrow* went out.

Matt and Charlie Foote were on watch the first night out. About one o'clock it was getting light, as is usual in Labrador. The mate told Charlie, "Go and call the skipper because we're getting pretty close here." They were going eleven knots when the skipper said to the watchmen, "Look here, by the looks of that land there is plenty of water here." The vessel was loaded in the forward hold, with nothing in the after hold, so she was down on her nose.

Matt was at the wheel when she struck. He recalls, "She took forty feet of the keel and the stove aboard was in the wing, that was over on the other side. The engineer, Lloyd, he was chief, he came full astern on the two engines but it never budged her. First we went out and sounded and there was all kinds of water. You know what, I believe it was the only rock around there because there was hundreds of feet of water all around it. So we took the anchor and carried it back with the dory and dropped it. Then we come on the anchor, hove her tight and come astern but she still won't come off."

In the meantime, the nurses were still on board and the skipper asked Matt to take them ashore and call on Captain Iversen, who was in the *Nellie Cluett* in the harbour. Matt landed at the back of the island in the dory. He and his passengers walked up over a hill and spotted a little house where smoke was coming out of an old stovepipe. The homeowners welcomed them and obligingly gave them a meal. Matt asked the man if he would take him aboard the *Nellie Cluett*. After being told of the *Silver Arrow*'s predicament, Captain Iversen exclaimed, "My God, I don't think that I can do anything out there with him. He'll never get off that."

While Matt went back to rejoin the nurses, Captain Iversen went out to the *Silver Arrow*. The crew had moved the salmon from the forward to the after hold until it was full, then put the rest on the quarters. Still the ship would not budge off the rock. Finally, when the tide came up they managed to free her. After getting into Packs Harbour and loading more salmon, they started back down the coast and dropped the nurses off at Salmon Bight.

The fellow who was buying their salmon was short of money for the last load. Arthur Earle, who was on board, told the crew, "Boys, you won't get out of Battle Harbour over the weekend. I haven't got a cent of money for this load of salmon. Until the money is in the bank in Carbonear, you don't sail." Sure enough, as soon as they docked Arthur jumped off the ship and headed for the Customs House to stop the ship leaving until the bank opened on Monday. He succeeded and it was only when a wire from Carbonear confirmed the money was in the bank on Monday morning that the *Silver Arrow* was cleared and could leave for Sydney.

They had a good southwest breeze of wind on the way but she did not seem to be making any time. When they got to Sydney, they discovered they had gone over a cod trap and had towed its leader all the way from Labrador. The vessel went on the slip in Sydney to assess the damage. With forty feet of her keel gone, the only thing that had kept her afloat was the cement along the keelson. As Matthew says, "If that would have broke, she would have went down like a rock, and her loaded besides."

While they were dry-docked in Sydney, Matt and Joe went to a show. When the movie was over they headed for the Grant Hotel, which was into bootlegging and where a drink of rum was twenty-five cents. To evade police raids, the proprietors would put their patrons in a special room. Matt and Joe went up to one of the rooms. While they were having their drink, there was a commotion going on next door. They recognized the loud voices as coming from two of their crewmen. In his inebriated state, one of them was demonstrating what he would do to Arthur Earle if he ever saw him again. While swinging he accidently struck his buddy and the fight was on until Joe came in to separate them.

After that the *Silver Arrow* went fresh fishing on the Banks off Nova Scotia. She was refitted in Pleasantville on the LaHave River. After a couple of years Captain Richards accepted a charter to go south in the banana trade. Matt told the captain, "I'm not going. I want to go fishing." Since he had a full crew for the trip south, the captain accepted Matt's departure "finest kind," indicating his general approval.

## The Pasadena II

Matt got his next chance with Captain Cecil Walters in the *Pasadena II*. In the summer of 1935 they went salt fishing, but the fish were quite scarce that summer and they averaged a couple of quintals (about two hundred pounds) short of what was considered a successful trip.

They went into Cape Broyle to see a fellow there who used to tow the dories out for squid. He invited the crew ashore on Saturday night for a taste of his moonshine. Some, like young Matt, were not particularly keen on drinking alcohol, but there were others who were "all gassed up" by twelve o'clock when it came time to return to the ship. When they were boarding the dories, Matt asked, "Where's my dory-mate?" The answer came back, "He's not coming." Matt shot back, "What's going on?" In reply someone warned, "There's going to be trouble tonight. We best get aboard fast." Nothing more would be revealed until the next morning.

It was raining and some of the crew spotted Captain Moyle Crouse from the *John W. Mackay* approaching in a dory. "Hauling her right to the painter straps," Matthew recalls, "he came aboard and he come down and went right to Cecil. Now Cecil Walters was a fine man and he wouldn't have nothing to do with anything."

The two captains had quite a little set to after Moyle accused Cecil of sending one of his crew to board his vessel and

A line of dories preparing for the day's work.

steal his trawl. Cecil assured him that if one of his men had done that it was entirely without his knowledge.

Captain Crouse calmed down after it became apparent that the perpetrators were two of the crew from the *Pasadena II* who had acted on their own after sampling moonshine in Cape Broyle. The story circulating was that one had coaxed the other into going aboard the *John W. Mackay* to steal the trawl. The thief had managed to get a load ashore and might have gotten away with it had he not been recognized by a fellow Newfoundlander while on board. The skipper and his crewman had given chase in a dory. They caught up with the felon and hit him with a paddle but he still got away. So they went to the police.

The policeman went looking for the suspect and found him asleep in the moonshine maker's dining room. The two vessels were held up pending the arrival of a judge from St. John's, following which a trial was held in the moonshine supplier's parlour. The defendant pleaded that his host had made him drunk with moonshine then promised to pay him a certain price per tub if he would steal the trawl and dory paddles from the *John W. Mackay*. He won his case and was cleared of all charges. The moonshine maker did not fare so well: he was sentenced to seven or eight months in penitentiary.

Next the *Pasadena II* was bound for Sydney. Matt's recently acquitted dorymate was all dressed up as they were coming into the harbour. He asked Matt, "Dorymate, aren't you going to get ready to go ashore?" Matt answered, "I got no money." His buddy replied, "I got plenty." It would seem his being found innocent of stealing had not compelled him to return the proceeds of the heist.

## THE DOT AND HELLIE

Matt's next opportunity was with first-time skipper Captain Loren Ritcey in the *Dot and Hellie* with Wallace Gaulton as dorymate. They fished all winter. While they were tied up in Lunenburg in the spring, Captain Richards returned

Teddy stands guard over tubs filled with trawl lines on the *Marguerite B. Tanner* docked in Sydney, Nova Scotia.

from the banana trade. He asked Matt to come back with him but Matt refused. His former skipper told him to sleep on it, warning, "If you don't come back with me you'll have to go back to Port aux Basques. I'll deport you out of the country."

Unbeknownst to Captain Richards, Captain Cecil Walters had helped Matt obtain his legal landing papers while he was working on the *Pasadena II*. Matt had left the legal documents with Harry Zwicker for safekeeping and they remained stored in the safe at W.A. Zwicker's clothing store. Following the encounter with Erlin Richards, Matt went to retrieve his papers from Zwicker's safe. Harry suggested to Matt that he not produce them until he was asked to do so.

The next morning Captain Richards, flanked by an officer of the Royal Canadian Mounted Police, picked Matt up and took him to Halifax to appear before Immigration authorities. When the official asked Matt if he had enough money to go back to Port aux Basques and then return to Canada legally,

Matt responded, "I don't think that I have to do that, sir." He then handed him the envelope containing his landing papers, all in good and proper order.

The ride back to Lunenburg with the Mountie and Erlin Richards was unusually silent. The Immigration official had not concealed his displeasure with Captain Richard's ill-conceived intervention. He chastised the skipper and counselled that it would be best to keep the incident quiet.

## THE BLUENOSE

In the fall of 1936, Matt and George Hamilton got a chance on the *Bluenose*. While on a trip the following February, they encountered a snowstorm packing hurricane-force winds from the northeast of some seventy miles per hour. They had to "lay to" for three or four days. One afternoon, someone coming back over the deck called out, "Did you see that vessel?" No one had seen it. Matthew remembers thinking, "How could anyone see anything in that storm!"

Then someone glancing to windward did see a ship: it was the *Keith Collins* and she was laying the same as they were until her skipper jibbed her over by putting her on the other tack. Matthew wonders to this day, "The name of God Almighty, now that was a close call too. She was right on top of us and we wouldn't have knew it if this guy wouldn't have seen it. He happened to come up from down for'd and looked to wind'rd, and in the snow he seen the black hull. She must have got around far enough that she went clear of us. We weren't doing anything, so when we went in Lockeport, George and I pulled out. We left that."

## THE BESSEMER

In the fall of 1938, Matt was hired on the *Bessemer* with Captain Tommy Himmelman to go halibut fishing. That winter, on Christmas day, there was a tragic accident which cost two men their lives. They were fishing on the Grand Banks but they were not catching much except from hand-lining off the deck and the weather was terrible.

Christmas morning there was no wind and the sky was right down on top of the water, a sure sign that a storm was brewing. The dories were dropped off with not much gear, only a dozen lines of trawl. The crew put out their trawl, hoisted their dories back in the vessel and came aboard. It was around ten in the morning and the cook blew the whistle for dinner.

The crew never did get to eat because by the time they got down to the table, the horn was blowing for them to "drop on" the dories again. As soon as they were back out in the dories, it breezed up and there came a snow squall. They hauled their trawl up as fast as they could, struggling against wind blowing at thirty miles an hour or more, and snow so thick they could not see their own hands. While they were making for the vessel, Matt and Pete Wells saw crewmates Al Ryan and Harry Keeping still hauling trawl. Someone from a nearby dory called to Al and Harry to come on. They answered they were hauling their buoys and only had one more line to get, or something to that effect.

Matthew reflects, "How in the name of God we got aboard nobody knows – we were only young. I told Pete, I guess this is it. Pete said that if we couldn't find the vessel we would go to Port aux Basques, that's where he was from. Anyhow, when we went down we made the vessel finest kind [without any problem], but we were going across her stern, and we heard her when she made a slat in the snow, rolling back and forth. When we let the dory come up, we came right up on the lee side of her. Don't you think that they didn't have some job to get us! The wind had picked up to fifty miles an hour or more and the vessel was jogging ahead so fast."

As fate would have it, they were the last dory to be picked up that day, around one o'clock. The *Bessemer* kept steaming around, trying to get up to where they figured the missing dory would be. The ship was bobbing up and down in hurricane-force winds, and after several hours of blindly searching the area, they were forced to abandon their efforts and head for home.

## CHANGING TIMES

Although cod, halibut and haddock had been the mainstay of the Atlantic fishery, in later years markets began to develop for flounder and perch. This required going to different areas of the Grand Banks: Green Bank, St. Pierre Bank, Stone Fence off the end of Quero, Banquereau, Middle Bank, Middle Ground, Sable Island Bank, Western Bank, Georges Bank, Brown's Bank and LaHave Bank. Brown's Bank had an area called Mitchell's Lump where later, when he was captain, Matthew always came away with a good set of fish. In the spring they went salt fishing up in the Gulf of St. Lawrence and Strait of Belle Isle, up around Cape North, and up on Bradley right up in the North Bay. "You were all over the place," Matthew says.

Matthew saw many fishing gear changes over the years. In the early days they used old cotton manila trawl, which would get pretty heavy when soaked and tended to drag over the bottom. The manila was also quick to rot and lacked in strength.

The nets had different parts: bottom belly, top belly, top and bottom wing. Most trips you had to change the bottom belly part because it was either torn or chafed as well as rotted out from dragging over the bottom. The wings lasted longer but also had to be replaced after seven or eight trips. Mending the nets was a challenge, but the crew would learn from each other and the more experienced men taught the novices.

In the salt fishing days, fishermen would go to the fish company's office for their pay. Some years they would have to wait until after Christmas for their money, till the fish was sold. Later on and into the 1960s, the captain would deliver each man's pay in a paper bag, and both captain and crew had to count out the money to make sure they had the right amount. Matthew recalls, "They had everything right much to the cent." It would be later, when they were paid from the fish

There was a time when men were paid according to fish count, not fish weight.

plant, that actual paycheques appeared. There were some exceptionally lean years during the Great Depression. One fellow told a story from his fresh fishing days whereby the captain jumped aboard calling, "Men come and get your money!" He then handed each man twenty-five cents.

There was a time when fishermen were paid according to fish count, not fish weight. Matthew explains the practice this way: "If you had a dory load of five hundred small fish and I had a load of one hundred bigger fish, you would be paid more for your load even though my fish was better."

This system was made even less equitable in light of the vast range in sizes of codfish. The smallest cod, or scrod, could weigh up to two pounds. "Market" cod ranged from two to seven pounds and "steak" cod weighed in at seven to ten pounds. Anything heavier was referred to as "whale" cod. One can only imagine how many fishermen may have drowned because of overloaded dories; the temptation to pack in as many fish as possible must have been great. One of the yarns circulating was of a fellow who used to roll an extra line of trawl around himself at night when no one would notice. In the morning when he was setting out his gear, he would raise his outside anchor and put the extra line on to get more fish.

In the 1940s there was still a lot of dory fishing, but change was imminent as indicated by trawlers showing up here and there.

## BOARDING HOUSES

Like many of his young unmarried Newfoundland shipmates, Matt would stay in Lunenburg boarding houses when in port. The one that left the strongest impression on young Matt was Margaret Flett's. At one time there were fifteen fellows from Newfoundland staying there.

Mrs. Flett had a full house of boarders in 1937 when the crews went on a strike that lasted some three months. Of course, the young men had no money and neither did Mrs. Flett. The captains had offered their crews to stay aboard their respective vessels for the duration of the strike while they were not being paid, because no one expected Mrs. Flett to feed her boarders for free. Yet to everyone's surprise, the lady had negotiated terms with Mr. Crouse from Kenny's grocery store whereby she could get all the groceries she needed on credit for as long as the strike lasted. So Mrs. Flett kept her boarders.

Matthew remembers asking her, once they were back to work, "How did you make out through being owed all that money?" Mrs. Flett replied, "Look, I got every cent back and more besides." This confirmed Matt's belief that those Newfoundlanders were a pretty good bunch of fellows. There were some fun times at Mrs. Flett's and lots of laughs. Although most everybody drank a little, things never seemed to get out of hand.

Jack Pink, one of the young men who boarded there, was friends with all his fellow boarders. He had done a lot of fishing with Captain Foster Corkum and despite his young age, Jack was offered command of the vessel when Captain Corkum passed away. However, he turned the offer down and opted to work on a freighter out of Yarmouth instead.

When Jack was driving back to Lunenburg for the weekend, the car he was in ran off the road and he was killed. His body was taken to Yarmouth and Sweeney's, who owned the vessel Jack had last worked on, provided the casket and arranged for a funeral and burial in Yarmouth. In spite of the fact there was precious little spare money around in those days, Jack's fellow boarders felt strongly that he should be buried in Lunenburg, since that was where he had spent his time while not at sea. Jack's friends pooled their resources and arranged for his body to be returned to Lunenburg. They accompanied the hearse to the train station to pick up the casket and escorted the remains to the funeral home. They had bought a burial plot on a hill in the Lunenburg cemetery and gave him a proper burial.

They wanted him to have a headstone so the group designated Matt to take up a collection. He went around to all the Newfoundland fishermen. Most gave a quarter or fifty cents, which was considerable since they were only making seven or eight dollars a fishing trip. A few gave a couple of dollars.

Matthew says, "If I had been collecting from all the skippers and everything I could have got a monument sooner because they all wanted to give me money. I wouldn't take it because I wanted something that we wanted to do ourselves. The only exception I made was for Mrs. Flett, who insisted on giving five dollars. Eventually I collected $219. Reverend Fowler, the Anglican minister, came with me to Bridgewater to pick out the headstone. It cost $185 and it is beautiful even today." The inscription on the headstone reads, "Donated from his Newfoundland Fishing Comrades and Mrs. Margaret Flett."

The remainder of the money collected went to pay a balance outstanding for the funeral expenses and toward pictures that had been taken to send to Jack's mother. Many years later, sometime in the '70s, Matthew was at home eating supper when Jack's sister and her husband appeared at the door. He took them to see the grave and they were most thankful for what had been done for Jack.

## MEDICAL CARE

In the days of sailing fishing vessels, an ongoing threat to a fisherman's welfare was sickness or injury. Matthew says, "If you got sick aboard, you had to be pretty sick for them to bring you in. You didn't have nothing aboard. Anything Epsom salts, iodine or Friar's Balsam couldn't cure, that was it."

Matthew poignantly remembers the curse of recurring boils, "water pups" they used to call them. They would grow on his arms, caused by friction from oil clothes and coarse sweaters, and would harden from the seawater. Finally one time, when suffering from water pups that had appeared in more intimate places, he went to a doctor in North Sydney. The doctor gave him a prescription, assuring him, "When you drink this you won't be bothered with any more boils."

Matt was skeptical but nevertheless he and his buddy Ira Durnford went to the drugstore to pick up the prescription. Between the two of them they managed to come up with the five or so dollars needed to pay for the tiny bottle, a considerable sum in those days. In spite of his skepticism Matt drank the elixir and sure enough, he was never bothered by boils again. Matthew comments, "Any fisherman would give their eye teeth for what was in that bottle!"

In between trips Matt had seen Dr. Creighton in Lunenburg a number of times for recurring sore throats due to tonsillitis. On the last visit, Doc had said, "Next time you're in port, we'll take those out." Due to the nature of a fisherman's lifestyle, doctor's appointments could not be pre-scheduled – you just showed up when you could.

Matt went to his office the next time he landed in Lunenburg. He sat in the waiting room until his turn came, then the nurse called him and brought him to the doctor's examining room. Finally, Dr. Creighton appeared. He examined Matt's throat, then handed him a metal surgical instrument some eight inches long, shaped like a hockey stick. He told Matt to use it to hold down his tongue and proceeded to coat the throat surface with an anaesthetic ointment. With surgical clippers, Doc reached in and gripped the first tonsil, which he snipped off and flung in a waste- basket, saying, "There, there's one." Then he repeated the procedure for the second tonsil. To Matt's uneasy surprise, he reached into his mouth again with the clippers, remarking, "Your palate looks a little long." He then proceeded to clip a piece of it off.

When he was done he coated Matt's throat again with a disinfectant and instructed him to lie down for a while until he came back to check on him. When Dr. Creighton returned he declared the throat looked good and told his patient he could go home, adding, "But don't eat any cornflakes for breakfast."

Much later in his career, when he had moved to trawlers and was fishing on the *Cape North* under Captain Tom Pittman, Matt would experience a medical emergency. He was working with his shipmates at taking the fish out. On his way down to the hold, as he stepped off the ladder, something grabbed his right side, causing him to double over. Soon, however, the pain had passed. After they had completed their work, Matt decided he should see a doctor.

Perry Conrad, who was mate, accompanied him to the marine hospital in Sydney Mines. The doctor there diagnosed appendicitis and wanted to operate on the spot. Matt protested, "No, I'm not getting it out here, I'm going home." The doctor instructed Perry, "You go back and tell the captain not to take this fella to sea like this." Back aboard, the skipper asked Matt what he planned on doing. Matt told him, "Going home." When Captain Pittman asked him how he planned to get there, seeing as there was a railroad strike, Matt answered, "I don't know."

Meanwhile, there were two men on the bridge standing nearby who overheard the conversation and walked toward them. Matt recognized one of them as being Mr. Adams from the American Consulate in Halifax, who had been on board on a previous trip. The other man was revealed to be Mr. Willoughby, the American Ambassador to Canada, who was visiting from Ottawa. Mr. Willoughby said to the captain, "We're going to Halifax in the morning. If he wants to come along we'll take him with us." After it was agreed, the ambassador told Matt, "You be at the Isle Royale Hotel in Sydney tomorrow morning. We'll be leaving around eight o'clock."

Matt showed up at the appointed time and place and waited in the lobby until Mr. Adams came to tell him they were ready to go. When they went out to the car, Matt was surprised to see a lady sitting in the front seat next to Mr. Willoughby. Matthew recalls, "At the time I didn't know his wife was with [him]. I thought it was just him and Adams." Matt was introduced to Mrs. Willoughby and took his place in the back seat of the Buick convertible. Since it was a lovely day with just a soft breeze, coming up around the Bras d'Or Lakes, Mr. Willoughby pushed a button and the roof folded back to let the occupants bask in the sunshine.

In those days, before the Canso Causeway linked Cape Breton and mainland Nova Scotia, you crossed the Strait of Canso by ferry. On the way across, Mrs. Willoughby decided she wanted something to eat but her husband said, "No, we're going to wait until we get to Antigonish." Once across Mrs. Willoughby took the wheel and her husband joined Matt in the back seat. Matthew reminisces, "We had the big yarn of course talking about the fishing and the building of boats. He was wonderful interested in the shipbuilding, wooden boats and that, and being that Lunenburg was a wooden shipbuilding town he done a lot of questioning me on that."

When they reached Antigonish they drove up to a hotel. As they got out of the car, Matt pointed to a Chinese restaurant across the street and told Mr. Adams, "I'll go over there and get a little something to eat." Mr. Willoughby overheard him and said, "No, you're not. You're coming with us." So they all entered the hotel and after freshening up they went into the dining room. Matt was feeling nervous but looking back he says, "There was no need to be – they were very down-to-earth people. They were easy people to eat with and they were easy people to talk with."

Coming into Halifax, before they reached Bedford, Matt told Mr. Adams, "You let me out when you get down here to a filling station. I can look after myself from there." They stopped at a gas station but Adams told Matt, "Sit still. I'll look after it." Then he gave Mr. Willoughby directions to his house in Dartmouth. Coming into Dartmouth, once again Matt tried to take his leave, saying, "Why don't you run me down to the ferry and everything will be okay." Again Adams answered, "No, you're coming up home. You have got to meet my wife." The Willoughbys also had not met Mrs. Adams so when she appeared holding a baby, there were introductions all around.

The Adamses invited everyone in for a drink. Matt recalls, "We got in the room and after a while we got into the big yarn and had a couple of drinks. Next thing a lady came and said dinner was being served. Then I had to go there and eat with them again yet. It was no problem – they were the kind of people that made you right at ease."

During dinner Mr. Willoughby said he would love to go to Lunenburg to see the shipyard and asked Matt if he would show him around. Of course Matt said he would. Mr. Willoughby said he might have to return to Ottawa in the morning, but if he had the time, he would come over, and asked Matt for his telephone number. Matt didn't have a telephone at home but had memorized the tourist bureau number so he gave him that. After dinner Matt asked Mr. Adams if he could get him a taxi. When he went out and got in what he thought was a cab, he found it odd the driver was wearing a uniform. When they got down to the ferry terminal and Matt went to pay the driver he said, "It's already paid for. I work for the American Consul."

Coming across the harbour on the ferry from Dartmouth to Halifax, Captain Frank Green recognized Matt from Matt having been on Captain Pittman's ship. They struck up a conversation and Matt told him his story. Captain Green offered to drive him as far as Queensland, where he lived, and from there Matt got another ride to Mahone Bay.

Matthew recounts that while he was walking along the road in Mahone Bay, "Who should come along but Dr. Hewitt, just the fella I wanted to see. He picked me up and said he had to make a call. He told me to come down to the office after a little while to see what was going on."

After Dr. Hewitt examined Matt he said, "There's nothing wrong with you, you're the finest kind [perfectly well]. You had the attack of appendix all right. It might never bother you again, but where you're going to sea all the time, I advise you to get it out. It could happen again at anytime. Perhaps the next time you mightn't be so lucky."

Matt agreed. It was a Saturday and Dr. Hewitt arranged for him to have the surgery the following Monday morning in Bridgewater.

On Tuesday morning, Dr. Creighton dropped by Matt's hospital room to see how he was feeling. Surprised to see him Matt said, "Pretty good. How do you know what happened?" Doc answered, "Oh, I flicked it out." Then he told Matt to get ready to leave later that morning. After he and Dr. Hewitt were finished their surgeries, they would drive him back to Lunenburg. Matthew says in amazement, "They brought me home yet!" Matt would have to be off work for five to six weeks.

One day during his convalescence, Matt was sitting on the curb on Montague Street with Len Fralick, a fellow fisherman, who was saying he also had recently been in hospital. All of a sudden, in mid-sentence, Len fell over, apparently unconscious. Matt walked up one block, as fast as his recent surgical wound would permit, to the nearest doctor's office. Dr. Cantalope happened to be coming out of the building. Responding to Matt's urgent beckoning, he covered the steps back to the fallen man at a brisk pace, Matt trailing behind. Unfortunately, Len could not be revived. Dr. Cantalope pronounced him dead at the scene, of an apparent heart attack. Dr. Saunders, who was coroner at the time, called at Matt's house as part of his investigation into the fatal incident.

# CHAPTER 3

# PUTTING DOWN ROOTS IN LUNENBURG

## A FISHING, SHIPBUILDING TOWN

During the Great Depression, Lunenburg had been a magnet for young men from Newfoundland who wanted to work on vessels that sailed out of Nova Scotia. The Lunenburg young Matthew Mitchell adopted as home was a busy town. At times there could be about a hundred sailing vessels in port. While ashore, the crews made the streets of the town come alive day and night. There was no shortage of shops of every sort and they all stayed opened late into the evening. The three main arteries in town – Lincoln, referred to as Main Street, Pelham and Montague Streets – featured the majority of the commercial establishments.

On Lincoln Street alone, there were five butcher shops: Berringer's, Gow Heisler's, Wamboldt's, and two others owned by the Hatt brothers. Main Street was also the stage for Zwicker's clothing store, Zwicker's Variety store, Younis' Buy and Sell, Harold Burn's ice cream parlour, Crouse's bicycle shop, Charles Oxner's barber shop, Himmelman's jewelry store and MacKay's bakery. Alex Sordero, Bertie Oxner and Kenny Crouse ran grocery stores on Main Street. Main Street also had Kinley and Fulton's drugstores and Mr. Wong's Chinese restaurant.

Pelham Street featured two bakeries – Ellison Corkum's and Mrs. Emeneau's – two grocery stores – Smeltzer's and Gibby Corkum's – Amos Crouse's blacksmith shop, and the Royal Bank.

Montague Street was the address for Dauphinee's Block Shop, which manufactured and sold equipment for vessels, such as blocks, paddles and trawl tubs, and Power's large retail store, which specialized in metal objects used in ships. Power's were internationally famous for their "double patent" horns. Montague Street was also home to Acadian Supplies, where coal and lumber was purchased for vessels, Tommy Walter's blacksmith shop and Beck's barber shop.

King Street fronted two banks, the Commerce and the Bank of Montreal, and Archie Morash's fishing supply store where fishermen bought items such as gloves, hook sets and tobacco. There were also businesses on some of the side streets, like Tom Lee's Chinese laundry on Cumberland Street and Mrs. Morash's grocery store on Prince Street.

In addition, all the fishing firms had their own general store. "So long as you were in their vessels you didn't have any problem to get anything," Matthew says. "You'd get your rubber clothes and gloves, whatever you wanted. But they were very tight on money. If you wanted five dollars and went to the office, you had to probably go to half a dozen heads before you could get that."

As Mrs. Flett had experienced during the strike, most storekeepers were generous when it came to giving fishermen credit. However, as one fellow who could not get out shore fishing due to bad weather found out, there were always exceptions to the rule. When he went into a store looking for a loaf of bread on credit until his next trip out, the shopkeeper told him, "I don't give no credit." The Lutheran minister happened to be in the store. He gave the fisherman ten cents, saying, "Go over to the next store and buy the bread."

In addition to seagoing vessels, there was a considerable amount of shore fishing activity around Lunenburg that entailed a large fleet of dory schooners. Mostly before Matt's time, there were a number of vessels with single dories, like the *Gloria May* and the *Isabelle Corkum* belonging to Captain Eric Corkum and Captain Irving Corkum respectively. Matthew says, "Now that must've been a worse life again, one man out there. Two at least you could have a yarn, but with one man out there all day long in the dory ... They called it single dorying."

A number of fishermen had two- and four-dory schooners: Enoch Tobin, Aubrey Levy, Bert Bezanson, Warren Levy, and Cecil Spindler from the LaHave Islands. Captain Orlando Lace had the *Astrid W.* and Captain Atwood Parks owned the *Kasagra*. Before Atwood Parks had the *Kasagra*, Captain Wilson Berringer had her out in a hard breeze of wind. Matthew recalls, "They figured that they would never see her no more. They claimed she laid like a duck you. They never wouldn't have lost even a trawl tub off the deck."

Of course there was lobster trapping, but there were also cod traps and cod nets around Cross Island and the Tancook Islands. In herring season the wharves and cold storage were full. Matthew remembers, "You could almost walk across the harbour on dories and boats full of herring in here landing. There was a lot of fish landed here from the shore boats and cod traps. Some years a lot of swordfish was landed here too and there was some tuna fishing here."

In the sailing vessel days, the salt fish would be landed to "fishmakers" all along the shores around Lunenburg. These fishmakers would wash off the salt, dry the fish and get them ready for shipping. The shores around Lunenburg and the LaHave River would be white with fish drying on flakes. Some of the fishmakers were the Allens, the Berringers and Bobbie Schwartz.

Matt helped land fish around the LaHave River, including Riverport. He recalls, "That was one of the hardest jobs, because when the tide was low, you had to fork them fish right up over your head, see. Then you had to help carry it in the store and they would all have to be salted over. On more than one occasion, there was a couple of men drowned landing fish out there in the river, I believe it was under the bridge there in Riverport. They had their dory so full and I guess going in the tide was running strong."

There was a place called Johnny Eisener's Hill between the town of Lunenburg and Blue Rocks where a number of captains had their homes. The Hill was home to Captains Guy Tanner, Tommy Himmelman, Leo Corkum, Joey Wentzell, Henry Winters, Lawrence Allen, Robbie Gerhardt and Aubrey Levy.

Matthew is not sure exactly how many vessels were around Lunenburg in the 1930s and the early 1940s, but he does know the local firms had dozens of vessels. Most of the crews came from Newfoundland and many of them would stay in boarding houses around Lunenburg then go back home around Christmas time for a month or so. During World War II many fishermen heading home for Christmas tragically lost their lives when the *S.S. Caribou* was sunk. On October 14, 1942, a German submarine torpedoed the ferry that plied the Cabot Strait between North Sydney, Nova Scotia, and Port aux Basques, Newfoundland, killing 137 of its 252 passengers and crew. Some of Matt's shipmates were among the men lost on the *Caribou*.

## An Acquaintance Meant to Last

While Matt was working on the *Pasadena II* in 1935, they came into Lunenburg for salt one day. The tide was low and the ship grounded off the wharf so they had to wait for high tide to sail away. While Matt was getting a meal at Wong's Chinese Restaurant, he met Olive Cook, who was working there. They would go together for a few years and marry in March 1939. Olive Cook was born in Feltzen South, one of nine children. Her mother was Almena Wagner and her father, Francis Cook, was a fisherman who went to sea for fifty years.

One time when Francis Cook was on the *Bessemer* on a rum run to St. Pierre, there was a sou'easter blowing and it was breezing up badly. The crew was called out to secure everything on deck. They had stopped the engine and were running off with the sails on her. Matthew relates what happened to his father-in-law that day: "He picked up a board on deck, a checker plank or something, and it blew and took him right overboard. She was running off before the wind and when he went back past the stern, they were towing a log in them days, and the log line went over his shoulder. He held fast to that and went right to the rotator. They let the vessel come up and they hauled him right in and he held fast. Four or five of them big men were aboard, a lot of them strong men, and they hauled him in, right in over the taff'l."

The first year Matt and Olive were married, they rented rooms in Charlie Lohnes's house in an area called The Battery about a mile from town. Snow removal could be problematic in winter. If a fisherman was home and available to shovel and did not show up for the task, he had to pay five dollars to Charlie for every storm. That was a lot of money at that time. Matt's landlord had hitched a plow to his oxen, which saved some shovelling, but there was still plenty of snow that had to be moved by hand. In those days heavy snowfalls were the norm and the shovelling was not limited to clearing your own road. In Matt's case, the proximity of his home to the marine hospital meant that nearby residents would pool their energies to clear the snow around the hospital as well.

A taxi ride into town was twenty-five cents, and since money was scarce, more often than not Matt would walk the distance in or out.

"I used to take a case of milk home on my back from out there in by the blacksmith's shop, Owen Smeltzer's," Matthew reminisces. "I'd go in and pick up a case of Carnation on my shoulder and go home just the same as if it was nothing. There was no post office out there – we used to get our mail through general delivery. We never had a telephone, nothing electric there; we had oil lamps and an old battery radio. There was no hospital here in Lunenburg, other than the marine hospital. Mrs. Knickle, she used to be the midwife, she would go around with the doctors in them times. My daughter Joan and my son Sherman was born at home. There was also a lot of babies born at Zinck's Nursing Home."

After a year or so the Mitchells moved to rooms in the back of town. They lived there for a few years until the rent got up to twelve dollars a month. Then it was time to buy a house. They bought Charlie Dauphinee's house in back of town. Matt had asked the old gentleman to give him first chance if he ever decided to sell. Charlie passed away while Matt was at sea but Charlie's children honoured the verbal contract. Matt and Olive were new homeowners.

Amongst their new neighbours were Captain Foster Corkum and Captain Eric Corkum, Captain Roger Conrad and Captain Bill Gilfoy. Captain Gilfoy gave Matt some old navigation charts and a seasoned half-quadrant for taking sights. He was also the first person to suggest to Matt he might want to learn navigation. The Mitchells lived at that address for some eight years, then bought the house on Linden Avenue where Matthew lives to this day.

## Balancing Time at Sea
## with Family and Community

Fishermen with bachelor status could go with the flow of the unstructured work schedule of going to sea at the pleasure of whatever skipper they served under. However, as a married man, Matt would face the challenge of balancing a career at sea with spending time with his wife and the children who would come over the years.

Usually fishermen could not afford a taxi ride to Lunenburg for just an overnight home when sailing from an away port like Halifax or Liverpool. Rather, they would make three or four fishing trips in a month, then go home for a day or two.

One time after they had landed in Liverpool, Matt and a couple of his buddies wanted to try Mackenzie's new bus line service to get home. The bus would take them as far as Bridgewater, but would only go on to Lunenburg if there were enough passengers to warrant it. For lighter loads, the company had purchased an old "three-seater" Packard, to serve the Bridgewater to Lunenburg leg.

That day, Matt and two friends and a lady passenger piled into the Packard at the Fairview Inn in Bridgewater headed for Lunenburg. Coming down a hill, one of the front wheels fell off and the driver was struggling to stop the car while his passengers howled with laughter. Matt remembers thinking, "If we would have died, we would have died laughing." The driver managed to bring the vehicle to a stop and called Mr. Mackenzie, who appeared in person in a brand new full-size automobile to drive them the rest of the way.

Halifax's Water Street was a pretty rough place in those days, renowned for its many bootleggers. A fellow they called Dirty John used to supply the crews with gloves and other fishing gear, although his store was more like a pawn shop than a general store. A few fishermen, when bent on going on a binge, would pawn their compasses, their dory sails, and anything else they could trade for money. Matt remembers being on a ship where there was only one dory sail on board.

While in port in winter, many of the fellows would spend hours at the theatre, where, for twenty-five cents, you could watch movies from eleven in the morning to eleven at night. Westerns were the favourite. Matt says, "Roy Rogers and Gene Autry and that bunch, there was nobody knew them better than us, I'm sure of that."

Halifax had a lot of Chinese and other nice restaurants, some featuring a dance floor. Fader's Drugstore on Coburg Road was a favourite stop for Matt and his comrades. The drugstore handled money orders, an essential service for getting crews' wages sent to their families. Fader's would go the extra mile for the fishermen. Matt recollects someone shopping for a bottle of perfume to take home to his wife for Christmas. A female clerk was helping with the selection while her customer squirted a little of this and that in search of the perfect scent. By and by, she pointed to a bottle, remarking, "Sir, this is called An Evening in Paris." The homesick fisherman replied, "I'd be satisfied for a night in Cherry Hill."

After a trip on the *Marjorie and Dorothy* that landed them back in Halifax, Matt and some of his buddies wanted to go home to Lunenburg. It was wartime and hiring a car was quite difficult. A couple of the crew were eating in a restaurant when a young man overheard them talking about wanting to go home. He told them, "I'll take you to Lunenburg. It'll cost you ten dollars." They agreed so the driver said he would pick them up at the wharf.

Back on board their vessel, the mate intercepted the fellows, saying, "Our fore-sheet block, she gave a clip and the side was broke out of it. You take that down to Dauphinee's Block Shop [in Lunenburg] and get it fixed for me." They said they would. Matt, Walton and two others were waiting on the wharf when the driver pulled up in a car sporting a flag on the aerial. Some of the fellows wanted to go for a drink but everything was closed. The driver said, "I can get liquor." On the way out of Halifax, he stopped at a house and returned with a quart of liquor.

When they reached Lunenburg, the passengers went their separate ways. Matt went home. The next morning he remembered the fore-sheet block and he went over to Walton's house to see if he might have it, but he had also forgotten to remove the piece from the car. Matt told his pal, "Look here, we're in for it. Laddie-o is gone, we don't know his name, or the name of his car, or the license. When we get back on board, we won't get a good reception."

They went back to Halifax and, of course, the first thing the mate asked them was where the block was. They had no choice but to confess. He told them, "We'll go up and find him. Where did you get him?"

Matthew remembers thinking, "What are we looking for? Unless we come right face on with him it would be useless, so we only just went to satisfy him. The mate was some put out over that and we were too because he entrusted that to us and we couldn't look after it for him. Yet I don't believe the skipper ever knew it. It never got to him."

On another trip home from Halifax, Matt found his house on Lawrence Street covered in bold yellow letters. Someone stopped him from entering and informed him the occupants were quarantined on account of having been exposed to diphtheria. While he wanted to see his family, Matt also wanted to continue fishing, so he headed downtown where he met up with a bunch of fellows who were drinking in the basement of the Ich Dien Hotel.

When he woke up the next morning, he was in his own house, now occupied by five women. So he found himself quarantined after all. They could only leave the house to swim in the back harbour or play ball in the field. The irony of it all was that samples taken from the allegedly contaminated person proved to be negative for diphtheria. It seems "quinsy," a rare variation of tonsillitis, was the culprit.

Friday and Saturday nights would see everyone converging on the town of Lunenburg. They came from First South, Bayport, Blue Rocks, Feltzen South and other surrounding areas. "If you wanted to see anybody and you went uptown on a Saturday night, you had no problem," Matthew comments. "If you never seen them all the week you would see them on Saturday evening. That's when they would do their shopping. The stores were open until eleven o'clock. Actually, the store might close around eleven but they'd still be there if you needed something.

"In them times you usen't to get home before Christmas Eve and you didn't have anything done. In the first place you never had the money to buy it ahead. You were just depending on them few dollars you would get that trip. You had to go and get a Christmas tree and whatever else you wanted. Then if you'd get a snowstorm yet it could mean delays or doing without."

Matthew remembers one year he arrived home on Christmas Eve with four dollars and eighty cents to cover all the holiday season expenses.

The price of admission to a dance hall was around twenty-five cents so there was no shortage of such facilities. In winter time dances might be staged in the schools or in some of the community organization halls. In summer they might be held in open-air sites, such as the Conrad property in Garden Lots. Matthew says it was a great place for dances.

Matthew doesn't recall any serious trouble around town attributable to liquor consumption at Christmas time or any other time of the year. He recollects, "In my earlier fishing days, we had wonderful cops: Tracey Knickle, and Goosey Gardner, they knew everybody. Anything they wanted you would do for them, but at the same time, if you come up and started acting up, instead of locking you up they would generally 'shoot you down' over the hill." Sometimes that literally meant kicking a fellow in the behind while they told him to get back aboard his ship.

"The odd time they would lock up a few fellows," Matthew says. "Then you know how bad they were now because anybody could walk in and out of the old jail on Montague Street. If you were working around the dock and sat down with a bottle of beer, they never bothered you, but if you got up around town with liquor they were pretty strict, everybody was wise to that. There was some bootleggers around too. They would raid them all the time. If they caught you with a bottle of rum on you, the fine would be sixteen dollars."

Election time meant a day off, a free trip home, and a lot of fun for fishermen. When J.J. Kinley was the elected Liberal Member of Parliament for Lunenburg, he would arrange for the fishermen in his riding to return home to cast their vote. Matthew remembers landing in Liverpool at election time and boarding a bus coming from Lockeport with other Liberal supporters on board.

One election time in Lunenburg, Matt and his friends, concerned about returning to their vessel in Liverpool, called on Mr. Kinley. He invited them in, handed out cigars, and told them, "No worries, my boys, we'll get you back." Looking after the voters was the order of the day. There would be "mickeys" of rum and cigars for the men and silk stockings and chocolates for the women, handed out by both major political parties.

Generally, if you had two dollars, you could get a taxi home from an away port. During the war, however, due to gas rationing, Halifax taxis were restricted to travel within twelve miles of the city. When it became increasingly difficult to get home, Matt was volunteered by his fellow fishermen from Lunenburg to drop in on an official at Government House to request a permit that would allow periodic trips home.

Dressed in his rubber pants, Matt announced to a secretary he needed to see the functionary responsible for issuing the permits. She told Matt, "He can't see you. He's at lunch." Now, on his way in Matt had spotted the employee in question sitting in his office with his feet up on the desk, reading a newspaper. He told the lady, "He's doing nothing, he's there." Matt kept insisting until she relented and had him admitted to the office. He left Government House with a duly signed pass in a sealed envelope.

Still, it was not clear sailing from there. "We had to do anything to get home," Matthew says. "You picked up whoever you could get to bring you down."

On one occasion when he and some other crew had left Halifax in an old car, they ran out of gas around Hubbards, not far from a gas station. The station attendant refused to give them gas unless they got permission from the Mounties to continue on their trip past six o'clock in the evening, as you needed clearance to do so. While Matt was on the telephone with the officer, the policeman asked to speak to the station attendant. They heard him tell the officer, "They look like fishermen. They're all dressed with leather boots and fishing clothes on." The officer must have been agreeable because he told the man to fill up the tank and give them oil if they wanted some. So they made it home that time but had to be back in Halifax the next morning.

On yet another trip home in an old car, Matt and his friends had hired a female driver. They were coming down a hill in Chester rather fast and one of the passengers commented, "We're bucking a heavy swell." Matthew describes what happened just as they got through the archway that frames the train tracks: "If it didn't go bang you! Look here, it was the same as a gun went off and the dust came up. This was the old tube tire and the tube come out and after a while it bursted. We had to go up to a garage and we had to go good on money for the tire."

Back in Halifax the next day, on Quinpool Road, the same driver "wasn't watching what she was doing and the car ahead stopped when he come up to the red light and if she didn't run into him." There appeared to be no damage, but the culprit saw fit to argue with the driver of the car she had hit until he flashed his badge: he was an RCMP inspector. With surprising composure he told her, "Lady, I'll take your license number and if there's any expense here I'll be billing you." They got back on their way and as they crossed the railway tracks in the south end, where boxcars were shunting back and forth, Matthew recalls, "Be damned if we almost didn't get run down by that. We just got across the bow of one!"

Fishermen looked forward to taking in at least part of the Fisheries Exhibition and Fishermen's Reunion from year to year. In the salt fishing days, the vessels would usually get in to Lunenburg on the eve of parade day. In the schooner days, they would have all of Exhibition week off and could take in all the activities.

In 1948, Matt, along with Venice Greek, Willis Randall and Hector Cook, all dressed in their oil clothes, carried Marie Hynes, Queen of the Sea, in a barrel chair with handles. With the chair hoisted on their shoulders, they crossed a field over to the building where the reception and dinner were to be held. The Queen's ninety-pound frame was but a light burden for these four strong young men.

Outside of the few allocated days off as dictated by the fishing companies, the only other holidays Matthew allowed himself from work occurred when he would pay someone to work for him on Good Friday and the day of his daughter Susan's wedding in 1975.

When Matt was fishing out of Halifax, there were travelling salesmen who used to come around the vessels selling their goods. One fellow peddled fabric, mostly blue serge. For ten to twelve dollars, you could get a piece of cloth large enough to make a man's suit. There was an excellent tailor by the name of Fred Loye in Lunenburg. He once made suits for both Matt and his wife from a piece of material that had cost less than twenty dollars.

The Hartt shoe salesman was popular with the fishermen, most of whom sported Hartt shoes. Matthew says he had a pair for years because they simply would not wear out.

One salesman who dealt in watches became an agent for Credit Jewelers. Matt was one of many who bought a watch by installment payments. Every purchaser would be given a buff-coloured card on which each payment remitted to the salesman would be recorded. Following Matt's last payment on the watch for Olive, his card was marked "paid in full." However, it appears there was a disconnect between the agent and Credit Jewelers because after his last payment, Matt received a letter from the company stating there was a balance owing on the watch.

He asked his wife, "You got that saved?" She answered, "Yes, I got that receipt." Olive was meticulous about keeping records. Matt told her, "Hold fast to it. We won't say nothing about it." He had heard the creditors were dropping in on some of his fellow fishermen, so he assumed they would soon appear on his doorstep. Sure enough, they did. The Mitchells produced their receipt marked "paid in full" and that was the end of it. Some of Matt's friends did not fare so well. Those who could not produce a receipt were deemed to be indebted to Credit Jewelers.

A significant percentage of the goods being peddled around the ships were acquired from stevedores who unloaded them. On a couple of occasions, Matt let himself be tempted by pieces of carpet. One salesman had persuaded him that he had the ideal rug for his kitchen. Since the salesman had noted the room's dimensions, there was no reason to believe it would not fit. He brought the carpet to the Mitchell house and rolled it out on the kitchen floor. It did not even cover half the surface. Fearing the sale was in jeopardy, the man stepped up his sales pitch but Matthew sent him packing, carpet and all.

The rejected dealer marched straight to the house across the street and sold the same rug to the lady of the house. Since Matt knew that his neighbour's kitchen was roughly the size of his, he felt he should tell her she had been swindled. The police were called and they caught up with the slippery salesman as he was leaving town. He was brought back and forced to return the lady's money.

Another time, a different carpet dealer showed up at the Mitchell home displaying an attractive Westminster rug. He rolled it out on the parlour floor, declaring, "You couldn't get a beautiful quality rug like this anywhere else for thirty dollars." Matt made him a much lower offer which was turned down flat. Matt then rebutted, "We don't want it. We're not interested." The salesman rolled up his rug and stepped into the kitchen where he rolled it out again.

Now Matt felt he had the advantage so he offered him twelve dollars. The man rolled the carpet up again and walked out to his vehicle. When he reached it he turned on his heels, came back to the house, threw the carpet on the kitchen floor and blurted out, "Give me the twelve dollars."

Matt held a driver's license for many years before he purchased his first automobile. He remembers going to Bridgewater for the driver's test. He thought he had blown his chance when the instructor chastised him for being too far over in his lane. Matt replied, pointing to the vehicle ahead of him, "That fella is over there." The instructor retorted, "Yes, if that fella goes out in the river are you going to follow him?" However, he got his permit and about a decade later, when he felt he could afford to pay cash for a new car, he bought a Ford Meteor right out of a showroom in Mahone Bay.

In spite of the scarcity of time on land, fishermen were known for volunteering their time for community projects. In the mid-1950s the Lutheran Church acquired some land around Lake Mush-a-Mush and wanted to build a church camp. The call went out to members of the congregation. Reverend Ball, the minister at the time, had drawn up plans for a large log cabin and carpenter Arthur Ernst was in charge of the building. Some of the men were assigned to the woods, where they cut trees with crosscut saws while others peeled and hauled them. Matt was part of the team who were peeling and hauling the logs up. In a single day, working from dawn until dark, they had the walls up and the roof on.

Many fishermen endeavoured to maintain ties with their community by belonging to various organizations. In 1945, Matt became a Mason. As well as the Masonic Lodge, over the years he belonged to the Eastern Star and the Orange Lodge. As a member of these lodges, he participated in many parades, notably on St. John's day. Each of the lodges held fundraising functions that welcomed the community at large, such as dances and luncheons or suppers. One such function Matthew joins in to this day is the fish chowder luncheon at the annual Lunenburg Craft Fair.

## Not Destined for the Army

Like many of the other men from Lunenburg, Matt was called up to go in the army when World War II broke out. Matthew recalls, "The time we went the old jitney [a wooden railway car] was here – she was right full you. There was a whole bunch of us fellas from Lunenburg."

A couple of weeks went by while the men were being tested and processed. Army officials were bringing the recruits in so fast they could not supply uniforms at the same pace. While the new recruits waited for uniforms and to be assigned their training destinations, a rumour started to circulate amongst them that so many fishermen were being called up, there would be no one left to fish. It seemed to the men who were still waiting that even though they had passed all the tests, all they did was shovel snow, since a snowstorm hit every day.

Matthew vividly remembers the events that would change his status: "I'll never forget it. It was in the morning – we were just after having breakfast. This big fella with more braid on him than when Churchill signed the Atlantic Charter come in and hollered out my name. He told me to follow him. I didn't know where I was going but I followed him. He put me in the office and told me to sit there, and that's all that was said. I set there and I knew where I was – I was in the doctor's office.

"A doctor come in and by and by a lady. She was an army woman too. Now I'll tell you, she was some size! They talked a little while and she asked me if I would like to be out of the army. Of course I answered finest kind. Then, instead of sending me home, I asked could they put me in the navy."

The imposing lady informed Matt the only place they were going to put him was fishing, then handed him his discharge. The discharge was conditional as he would continue to be called every six months. Even though his skipper would sign for an extension, Matt was called another time, but after a couple of weeks of waiting at the recruitment centre, he was released again. It would seem someone was pulling strings to make sure there would be enough fishermen left to fish.

# CHAPTER 4
# FISHING WHILE THE WAR GOES ON

## WAR RESTRICTIONS

During wartime, every ship entering Halifax Harbour was expected to report to the examination boat, which took the vessel's particulars of tonnage, nationality, cargo and the like. The navy then authorized the vessel to pass through the anti-submarine net, or gate, across the harbour. However, sometimes the task at hand would take precedence. Once Matt was coming into Halifax on the *Brenda Marguerite*. She was slightly ahead of the *Theresa E. Connor* and was maneuvering to be the first one in to land their fish, which would mean bypassing the examination boat.

It was not long before a loud bang was heard. Somebody on the *Brenda Marguerite* yelled, "Thunderation, what was that?" The man at the wheel yelled back, "If you don't stop, you'll know what it is next one!" Then seemingly out of nowhere there was a small boat alongside from which a note was handed to the skipper on the end of a long stick. The note read, "Report back to the examination boat." The *Theresa E. Connor*, who had reported for examination and received clearance, passed them on their way to the harbour to land their catch.

Another audacious skipper who was on his way out of the harbour had been instructed to lay just inside the gate to allow a convoy to pass, as convoys took priority. Instead of complying, he steered his vessel toward the outgoing ship in an apparent attempt to go out alongside. The security gate was swung across just in time to prevent him from passing. The wayward skipper's vessel got tangled in the gate and sustained enough damage to require the towboat escort back to the dock. Matthew marvels to this day, "It's a wonder he wasn't hung. He was a lucky man that he got away with that."

### THE MAHASKA

Early in 1939, before the war broke out and before his marriage to Olive, Matt and Mike Lundrigan were getting off the bus in front of the Ich Dien Hotel in Lunenburg, when they spotted Captain Orlando Lace standing nearby. They asked him if he was looking for any men. The skipper replied he needed a dory's crew aboard the *Mahaska*.

Taxi driver Oliver Levy took the two recruits to Halifax to collect their gear from an Irving Oil building on the waterfront. The usual gear consisted of a mattress, a pillow, a bag of clothes, trawl tubs, a gaff, a compass and a dory sail. A sea chest was not needed in fresh fishing; the only time Matt had carried a sea chest was while salt fishing on the *Pasadena II*. At any rate, the newer vessels were equipped with lockers.

On one occasion after Christmas they were ground fishing between Cape North and Cape St. Lawrence. Matt recalls, "It was a snowy day, wind nor'west and snow squalls. Sometimes in the squalls it would breeze up just about fit to be out in a dory. All of a sudden, we were around three or four dories from where the first dory was dropped. We had on our rubber clothes and an old stocking cap and a sou'wester over that."

When the sea hit one of the dories and turned it bottom up, Matt and his dorymate heard them holler. They turned in the direction of the shouting, parted off their trawl and rowed up toward the distress sounds. The tide and wind slowed their progress while the upturned dory was drifting with the men on the bottom. They finally reached the site and pulled Martin Green and John Ingram aboard. Meanwhile, those on the vessel had witnessed the accident and were steaming toward them. Back aboard the ship, Matt and Mike were rolling the rescued men face down on a barrel to force them to eject sea water. Matthew says, "Everytime you rolled, they would spew out a gush of water. That's the way we got them to." Jack Ingram would go on to live to a ripe old age, but sadly a couple of years later, Martin Green was lost on another voyage.

The day the war broke out, the *Mahaska* was returning from the Grand Banks that morning with a trip of halibut and thirty-five swordfish in her old bow. The swordfish were caught with darts shot by a man standing in an empty two-hundred-pound pork barrel nailed to the bow. When they landed in Lunenburg, there was no buyer for the swordfish and there was talk of shipping them. After the crew had cleaned the halibut, they went home for the night. On returning to the vessel the next morning, they heard the swordfish had been sold after all. Word was the load went for thirty-five dollars, a dollar a fish.

Another time on the *Mahaska*, while the war was on, they were fishing on St. Pierre Bank. It was a calm day with a breeze of wind some twenty miles an hour. After returning aboard without any fish, the dorymen spotted a vessel five or six miles to leeward. The captain decided that after he ate his meal, he would pay them a visit. He told Matt, "Take the wheel and keep her down for that vessel." When he came back from eating, he asked, "Where's the vessel?" Matt answered, "Down ahead." The captain looked. "I don't see her." Matt looked again and could not see her either.

Meanwhile, the crew were baiting around the cabin house. One of them jumped up and yelled, "Oh my God, here's a submarine!" It was wartime, so of course everybody panicked. There was a lot of shouting and begging the skipper to turn around and to go away. His response was, "What's the good for us to turn and go from that if it's a submarine? He'll have us before we get five miles away. We might as well go down and pay him a visit." As they got closer, they could see the

Aboard the schooner *Marguerite B. Tanner,* captained by Atwood Parks, in the 1940s.

bowsprit, so it could not be a submarine. As the *Mahaska* approached, Captain Arch Thornhill of the *Florence* hailed them to come aboard. Captain Lace, Burton Levy and Matt went aboard and were told what had happened.

The *Florence*'s dories were out and only the skipper, the flunky and the cook were on board as the vessel sailed back and forth. When she came around to go on the other tack, Matt recounts, "She came up in the wind, the forestays all parted and the two spars come out of her and came down right across the quarter and broke the quarter off her, so everytime she would make a roll, the water would gush in down there." When the dories came aboard, the crew were told to get their clothes and what gear they wanted to transport aboard the *Mahaska*.

The damaged vessel was beyond towing, so everyone abandoned ship. Matt and Burton were instructed to set fire to the *Florence*. "We went down forward and ripped open old

On the *Marguerite B. Tanner.*

straw sacks," says Matt. "Then we came up on deck and before lighting the torch, we got a dory load of stuff off of her.
We had the bell and she had a beautiful set of copper kettles,
we got that. We had a lot of new trawl and splitting knives because they were salt fishing. We had quite a lot of cut-throats
they called them at that time, otherwise it's rippers – they were
great knives. We had the middle of our dory full. We went to
work and lit a torch and threw it down." The damaged vessel
burned from noon or so until dark, burning right out before
she sank.

They took their guests to Sydney. At the inspection gate
in the harbour, a man on the examination boat hollered out,
"How many men do you have aboard, Cap?" The response
came back, "Forty-eight." The examiner then called, "How
many dories?" Captain Lace responded with "Twenty-two." He
was asked to repeat the number of men. Then the man on the
examination boat bellowed, "Where in hell do they all sleep?"
Matthew comments, "He had no way of knowing he was deal-
ing with a shipwrecked crew."

The first time Matt became acquainted with "flying and setting in the night," it was on the *Mahaska*. This fishing technique would be practised after a full day's work was already done. The dorymen would return aboard and each man would bait a couple of tubs of trawl. They would return to their dory with four tubs of trawl, which they set out one at a time. Then they would actually lay on the ends of the line until the vessel's horn blew the signal to start hauling the trawl in. By then they would likely be half frozen but would continue this operation all night.

On the *Mahaska*'s second trip to MacDonald's Bank for halibut late in the fall, some of their gear was out and they anchored. Somehow they lost their anchor. They had another one on board but it was missing its wooden stabilizing stock. They went into one of the harbours to look for a suitable stick to make a new stock, which would serve them well for the rest of that trip.

Traditionally, anchors had been secured with Basque cable, which was made of rope. This was changed in favour of wire cable and the result was many lost anchors. Matthew comments that the anchors were lost "hand over fist because there was no give there. Look here, with that kind of wire in a little swell when it come tight it would clip right off." Captain Lace devised a way to compensate for the wire's rigidity. He placed a boxcar spring between the anchor and the cable at the point where the anchor was shackled on. That put an end to losing anchors.

On another trip back from halibut fishing, the *Mahaska* was off Beaver Light, east of Halifax, when a loud bang was heard: the crankshaft had broken. Captain Lace wanted to call a towboat but the engineer insisted he could get her going once the engine cooled off. In this case, the flywheel was on the back end of the engine. Had it been on the front end, Matthew says, "You could've ran her but it was broke off on two cylinders. So what he done, he tore down and disconnected the front end and run her in on the four cylinders. She wasn't going fast but she was going. You couldn't come astern

Processing the catch.

on her so we had to be very careful getting to the dock. He got her in, though."

Once on a run to St. Pierre, the *Mahaska* went into Belleoram, Newfoundland, for bait. They had to stay in overnight for the bait to settle, so they planned to go to a dance that evening.

In the morning on the way out, the skipper told Matt and a couple of other fellows to get the dory ready. He called the crew on deck and told them, "Anybody wants any liquor, give those fellows the money." Then the captain took the vessel right up to Green Point in the harbour at St. Pierre and dropped the dory off. He told the trio, "When you're ready, come out and stick up the dory sail so I'll see you."

The vessel went out to wait at a distance for the dory to reappear. The dory crew went into St. Pierre and completed their errands, coming out with a doryload. Back on board they distributed the goods and the vessel steamed to about five miles off Gallantry Head, then stopped. There the captain told his crew, "Boys, if you want to drink anything, drink tonight, because if I see anybody with a drink tomorrow morning, the works of this will be dumped overboard." So they stayed there that night to party and went fishing on Green Bank the next day. They got a good trip of fish, which they landed in Lunenburg.

On yet another trip, the *Mahaska* was one of five vessels at Round Counter (Rencontre) in Fortune Bay, Newfoundland. That night the crew went to a dance. When they returned aboard, Matt remembers, "It was blowing a half gale of wind in from the sout'rd, right into the Bay. We figured, now this is a night in, when we got aboard." But Captain Lace would surprise them.

Matt recounts, "He hove up the anchor, let her come right out through. We went right out through that night, through hail, glittering, snow and everything else you, never stopped for nothing. But the skipper stayed there right until she got out past the mouth of Fortune Bay, then he put the course on her and he turned in."

One Sunday when they were fortunate enough to be in their home port of Lunenburg, the crew of the *Mahaska* were looking forward to a day off work. In the meantime, one of the owners of the *O.K. Service* had been negotiating with Captain Lace about taking on his 50,000 pounds of halibut. Captain Lace asked his crew if they would be willing to return at midnight to take the fish out. They all agreed and reported at the designated hour. They weighed the fish, cut the heads off, filled them with ice and put them aboard the *O.K. Service* – all free labour. By nine in the morning, the *O.K. Service* was going out the harbour bound for Boston. As Matthew puts it, "We done a lot of good stuff but they never give us much thanks for it."

On another trip, the *Mahaska* traded codfish for halibut with a Newfoundland vessel that was salt fishing. Every evening some of the *Mahaska* crew would go aboard and get a doryload of halibut and vice versa. When the *Mahaska* landed with their halibut in Halifax, the buyers claimed the fish were slit down too far, a tactic aimed at bringing the price down. As

Matthew muses, "What difference would that be, cut down an inch below the nape? They tried anything."

Once while the *Mahaska* was landing its catch in Liverpool, Captain Arnold Parks had run the *Bruce and Whyona* out on a sandbar. Captain Lace took his vessel out to assist. When the *Mahaska* came alongside the stranded vessel, it was close to shore and she rolled down on top of the *Bruce and Whyona* and cleaned the rail off her. Captain Lace was forced to abandon the rescue mission. By the time the stranded ship got off the bar, the engine was clogged with sand. The *Bruce and Whyona* had to be towed to Lunenburg and the engine had to be replaced.

One summer the *Mahaska* was halibut fishing on the Battle Shoals section of the Grand Banks. They were also taking codfish but were restricted to some 20,000 pounds to be salted because of having to store ice for the halibut.

There were usually Portuguese vessels anchored around Battle Shoals and since the *Mahaska* habitually had more cod than they could keep, they would give the surplus to the Portuguese. Their fishermen fished on count and one of them was relentless in his efforts to maximize his count. He would go from dory to dory and the crew would keep giving him the codfish. His count kept going up but this practice was causing his crewmates' tempers to flare. Finally, one of the Portuguese officers came aboard and told Captain Lace, "We appreciate the fish, but we are going to have a row on board if your fellows don't stop giving him the fish." The skipper asked him, "Do you want the fish?" When the officer answered, "Yes," Captain Lace proposed, "I'll tell you what we'll do. We'll save the fish on deck and you come aboard and you can divide them up whatever way you like."

Matthew reminisces, "We got to be pretty good buddies with them fellows. Every time we went down we would find them there, [so] we didn't have to go sounding around. When we were getting ready to leave, if we had any bait left, we would give them our bait and they would give us their mail."

The Portuguese fishermen had arranged for their mail to go to the Customs House in Lunenburg. The crew of the

*Mahaska* had taken it upon themselves to pick up and deliver their Portuguese comrades' mail while they were travelling to and from Battle Shoals. The Portuguese kept offering unlimited barrels of wine, but that was not the drink of choice of their Canadian and Newfoundland buddies.

Another time on the way down to the Grand Banks, there was a lot of bad weather and the skipper was not able to get a sight due to heavy fog. They came across an old square-rigged ship they knew would belong to a French fisherman. Matt and Phil Degushie were on watch and Captain Lace told them, "You fellows go aboard. We'll go here to windward and drop you off. Go aboard and get the latitude and longitude from them where they are." The two young lads went aboard the French vessel and when they got down in the cabin they realized no one aboard spoke English.

The captain led them to a large table covered by an enormous chart. Matthew remarks, "I think all the world must've been on it." The skipper was pointing to a spot on the chart, but Matt and Phil could only make out the odd word of what the Frenchman was explaining. Eventually, half inebriated from the wine their hosts had served, the two returned aboard the *Mahaska* without a position. Their frustrated skipper scolded, "I might've known better then to send you two goddamned fools aboard there." Their defence was, "Then nobody could talk to us [so] what could we find out?"

Matthew stayed with the *Mahaska* until 1941. Then the *Alcala II* was being launched and its command was offered to Captain Orlando Lace. Naturally, he wanted all of his crew from the *Mahaska* to follow him to the new vessel, which they did. Command of the *Mahaska* passed to Captain Lorraine Zinck, who had to go to Lunenburg to hire a new crew. After he went out on his first trip, stories circulated that he had lost two men. In fact, the two casualties were from Matt's hometown and one of them was his first cousin.

## THE ALCALA II

When Smith and Rhuland launched the *Alcala II* from their shipyard in Lunenburg, Matt was on board. He and some of his crewmates helped to rig her and fit her out, and were out on the trial spin. The first trip out, they left Lunenburg around two o'clock in the morning and went to Halifax for a compass adjustment. Matthew remarks, "The time didn't mean nothing in them days. Anytime at all you'd go."

On one trip in the *Alcala II* they were fishing down by Sable Island on Banquereau. It was a nasty evening, thick of fog, and a couple of dories from another vessel had strayed but they got them back. When the crew of the *Alcala II* were setting out their trawl in the morning, they realized how easily these dories could have been lost. While they were steaming up to get room to position all of their dories the way the tide was going, they came upon a lone dory. Someone commented, "One of our dories is there already" but it was not one of theirs. Matthew recollects, "These two fellas was astray you. They were all night in the dory. We put them aboard their vessel, a Newfoundland vessel. If we would have set the other way, we mightn't've seen them at all."

In the schooner days, 300,000 pounds of fish was considered a big trip. Matthew recalls the *Alcala II* landing 309,000 pounds of fresh steak cod. In Matthew's recollection, that was the biggest trip of fresh fish ever landed by a schooner. "We had her full in the hold," he explains, "and the buoy locker on deck full. When we were splitting them, me and Sammy Tanner, we were in the hold and we forked the whole bloody works. They were only taking them out through one hatch."

This was taking place at the same time as the new wooden side trawler *Cape North* was in with a load. They had splitters on the dock to split their steak cod. That season the codfish was plentiful and there were many vessels in port with loads of fish. The large catches required that the fish be split and salted as soon as possible.

## The Marjorie and Dorothy

After the *Alcala II*, Matt went with Captain Ornam (Ernie) Mossman in the *Marjorie and Dorothy*. They went fresh fishing out of Halifax all year around for Maritime National and General Seafoods. There not much money to be made but at least they were in port every week. Prices for haddock ranged from one and three-quarter cents to four cents, maybe five cents in winter. A fish trip that brought in twenty dollars in total was considered a good trip. Matthew recalls Captain Angus Tanner of the *Brenda Marguerite* landing 220,000 pounds of codfish for which it was said he received forty dollars. This was considered such a major event that reporters came aboard to record it.

It was unusual on a fresh fishing trip to go into Burin, Newfoundland, for a baiting of caplin, but once the *Marjorie and Dorothy* and the *Theresa E. Connor* with Captain Clarence Knickle went in there together. After they got their bait, they headed for the Grand Banks where the codfish proved plentiful. Captain Mossman wanted his crew to set out a lot of trawl but the fish was in such abundance it was impossible to keep the gear clear. In fact, after three days there was a fish on every hook.

Matt and his dorymate were coming down for the last time. Matt's dorymate was rowing and he kept going to sleep, causing their dory to steer a course straight at a nearby dory. Matt kept telling him, "Wake up and keep this thing on course or we'll have some snarls if we don't." They did make it back on board to find the deck full of fish from forward to aft, when there was only room for 50,000 pounds in the hold. Still sleep deprived, the dory crews dressed the fish and filled the vessel, hatchways and all. Yet a pile of fish was left on deck. The skipper would not hear of dumping them, so the crew, having doggedly worked for days without sleep, had to retrieve the fish from the hatchways and cut their heads off to make room for the entire catch.

One evening, when there was no wind but it felt like a hurricane was brewing, Captain Mossman took the vessel out of Halifax. Sure enough, it started breezing up from the southeast and they headed out for the Banks as the wind progressed from a breeze to a gale. By midnight there was quite a storm of wind. The skipper was in the wheelhouse when he noticed the foresail begin to tear so he hollered to the crew to come up and take it down. Whoever was at the wheel let her fall off so a squall filled the foresail and she blew away. Matthew comments, "She's going yet I imagine. It took it right out of the ropes altogether you!" The skipper was anything but pleasant when they were forced to go into Lunenburg to get another foresail.

They were out on another night Matthew describes as "one of the worst breezes of wind that ever I was in in my life." That night another ship, the *Arthur J. Lynn* with Captain Fenton Tanner, had its wheelhouse severed, and the captain and two other men were lost. The vessel was laying over with just the foresail, almost to the cabin house in the water. Matthew recollects, "Some dirty stuff come down that night. I'll tell you I was in some hard breezes of wind with Ernie Mossman."

## LAND INTERLUDE AT THE FOUNDRY

During World War II, when Matt was on the *Marjorie and Dorothy*, engine trouble forced the ship into refit for a two-to-three month period. Matt decided he would approach the Lunenburg Foundry for a job in the interim. He was interviewed by Dan Young and Charlie Young. Since Matt was a big, able fellow, they decided he might be a fine candidate for bucking rivets, so they offered him the job of "bucker." The beginning wage would be sixty cents an hour, but once he proved he could buck rivets, he would receive the regular bucker's wage of ninety cents an hour.

Matt reported to his job site on the slip and was handed the bucking tool, a big old piece of iron with one bevelled and one flat end. Matt describes the bucker's job: "I used to put that on, they'd shove the hot rivet in, and then I would put that on for that fella with eighty pounds of pressure in there and have to hold that." It was the bucker's responsibility to keep the rivet tight to the shell plate to prevent the rivet head from being deformed during driving.

Matt became good friends with the navy inspector, a fellow by the name of Appleby, whose job it was to inspect all the rivets. He indicated Matt was doing a pretty good job considering the tool he had to work with, and he told management so in the hope the promised wage increase would materialize. However, the raise was not forthcoming.

Meanwhile, a ship that was missing its bow came in and they sent for a rivet driver from Pictou who was also qualified to fit steel plates. Dan Morrison was one of the union leaders in Pictou and was used to working with the best equipment. He was aghast at the tool Matt had been given as bucker and promptly ushered Matt to the Foundry office, where he produced a long list of tools and gear they would require to do the job. He taught Matt to drive rivets so well, in fact, that he told him, "Look here, you done a wonderful job. I'll take you on any riveting gang in the country."

After Matt had been on the job over two months, he told his mentor one morning, "Dan, I'm going to leave." Dan replied, "I only got a little while here. I thought you should stay while I'm here." So Matt told him he had not received the bucker's wage he had been promised. Dan asked him to be patient a few days more, that he would get his rightful wage. However, it would not go as smoothly as Dan had forecast.

Matt had to repeat that he was leaving, this time to Charlie Young. Finally, Dan's argument that it made more sense to keep Matt at ninety cents an hour than to bring someone in from Pictou at over a dollar an hour prevailed and Matt got his raise, complete with back pay. In the end he stayed until Dan Morrison's time was up in March, putting in a lot of overtime, as many as 113 hours in one week alone.

While at the Lunenburg Foundry, Matt worked on several ships, many of them involved in the war effort. One of them was the *Naomi*. She was to be "shoved off" one morning and the Foundry workers had toiled all night taking out tons of water that had been put in to test the tanks. When morning came, there remained some eighty tons of water aboard on one side of the boat, but the inspector ordered her shoved off anyway. Matthew recounts, "They shoved her and she just got the length of herself when she broke down the slip. She went right over on her beam ends.

"There was a whole bunch of us aboard her. We had to go to work and take everything off of her, everything that was moveable; we were a day or two at it. There was a big ocean towboat came from Halifax to tow her off. It had to be at midnight – that was when the tide was going to be high to try her.

"They got a big hawser, a heavy line aboard and tied it fast. There was a Navy man from Halifax with a lot of brass on him giving the orders. When he give the orders to tighten her up, he went out and took a strain on her and he never budged her. He hollered to the captain of the towboat through a loudspeaker. I don't know what was said but I heard him holler back, 'Brace your feet.' He backed her right back to the slip, right back alongside, and he must've rung her on full speed. If she wouldn't have came I don't know that she wouldn't have broke in two. She went with a jump and she rolled rail in and rail out, rocking back and forth." Then a smaller towboat came and took her to the dock while the ocean towboat went back out to sea.

### BACK ON THE MARJORIE AND DOROTHY

Malcolm Crouse, the engineer on the *Marjorie and Dorothy*, was being paid twenty-five cents less than the going rate, which was one dollar a day. In addition to wages, engineers also received their share of each trip. Malcolm was considered well qualified and had been asking for wage parity with his peers. When he did not receive the extra quarter, he decided to take a trip off. A fellow who stood watch with him in the engine room stepped in for that trip.

The *Marjorie and Dorothy* left Halifax heading for St. Pierre Bank, expecting to get there the next morning. Supper was around 3:30 in the afternoon, and following the meal

Captain Mossman announced, "We'll bait up and be ready for the morning."

Everything went like clockwork and after they had baited up the crew settled down around a chest in the cabin for a game of poker. Suddenly, the engines slowed down. The stand-in engineer and his helper, a very short fellow sporting a rag in his pocket that hung down to his heels, managed to get the engine going again, but only at low speed.

The crew thought they would never get to the Bank. Once there they managed to fish their trip and started for home. Matthew describes their journey: "The name of good God Almighty, there were times that she was barely moving, then she would speed up a little. Finally, we got in off George's Island in Halifax. All of a sudden, she went a-davie – stopped cold. Somebody had to shove us into a dock."

The agent for the Fairbanks Morse Company came down to the dock but after looking things over he was not able to start the engine up while the boat was docked. He said to the skipper, "There is nothing wrong with this engine."

Captain Mossman, adding a few expletives, repeated, "There's nothing wrong with this engine?" The agent added, "I should have her running loose. I can't do nothing with her here to the dock. I'll start her up for you [away from the dock] and you go to Lunenburg and send for Jim Young from the Foundry."

So they left for Lunenburg. Matthew recalls, "The name of God Almighty you, she never went better in her life. She was making her ten knots coming up. The best of it was we were coming in Lunenburg Harbour and Captain George Himmelman was coming out in the *Lila B. Boutilier*." When Captain Mossman tried to slow his engine down coming inside The Battery, he could not. He rang the bell to summon the engineer. A couple of the crew grabbed the wheel and hauled her hard over. The agitated skipper said, "We've got to go back to sea – we can't get her stopped." Finally, they had to turn the fuel off; when the fuel burned out of the line, the vessel stopped. Then Captain Himmelman took them back to the dock.

Jim Young came down from the Foundry and repeated the maneuvres the fellow had done in Halifax. He also told the captain, "Mossman, there's nothing wrong with your engine." Then he asked, "Who's your regular engineer?" The captain answered, "Malcolm Crouse."

Jim urged, "Get him in here." Malcolm Crouse showed up the next morning dressed in a suit, hat and all. Captain Mossman asked him, "When are you going to fix the engine?" Malcolm answered, "There's nothing wrong with the engine."

The skipper started cursing, irritated by the now too familiar answer. He asked the engineer, "When can we go?" Malcolm replied, "Whenever you want to go." The captain decided, "Okay, then we'll go tomorrow morning, but I'm still doubtful." So Malcolm told him, "I'll tell you what we'll do. When we pass Cross Island tomorrow morning, if this thing isn't running the same as she always did, you can bring me back and land me."

The next morning they fitted out. Going out of the harbour, Matthew recollects, "She was clinking and snorting and slowing down and speeding up and slowing down and so on. Mister, after a while he got her tuned up. The name of God, man, she was her old self. She was out of time, see. They couldn't time her to the dock – she had to be running free. That was the reason. It's just Mossman couldn't get it in his head." After that, Malcolm finally got his twenty-five-cent increase.

On another occasion during the war they were on the way to the Grand Banks when the vessel broke down. They were about eighty miles abeam of St. Pierre and this time the problem was a piston. They rigged up sails wherever they could fit them and sailed some eighty miles into St. Pierre. Of course the war was on and the harbour boats would approach every ship as if it were German. The *Marjorie and Dorothy* cleared security and found a Frenchman in St. Pierre who fashioned a piston out of hardwood. In fact, he made a spare in case one would not complete the trip. However, the engineer was not agreeable to using the wooden piston, so one was ordered from Lunenburg to be delivered to Sydney.

While laying off St. Pierre, the liquor had been flowing like water. They came into Sydney with an abundance of liquor on board. It got so that even the policemen in Sydney were partaking of the ship's generous hospitality. One of the policemen's wives came down to the vessel and told the skipper, "If you don't get him off there, I'm going to get the Mounties to come down and raid you." So the captain took the liquor off the ship and put it in the cold storage.

The *Marjorie and Dorothy*'s troubles were not over yet. When the new piston arrived in Sydney it did not fit. They had wasted about a month's time since the breakdown. When they finally got underway, coming out of Sydney, the skipper ordered the annual dumping of the ballast on the way to Lunenburg for refit. When the designated crew went down in the hold, they found a couple of their crewmates drinking out of jugs down there. Having been found out, the culprits wasted no time hauling out the ballast. Captain Mossman was later heard saying that was one of the hardest trips he had ever taken.

Captain Ernie Mossman had a reputation for "getting the sayings off," as Matthew puts it. One time going through the Gut of Canso, the examination boat came up to them and was grilling Captain Mossman with all kinds of questions. When the examiner was finally done, skipper Ernie's parting shot was, "We're a bunch of Dutchmen and Newfoundlanders and we had sauerkraut for dinner!"

The *Margaret K. Smith*, a Lunenburg vessel owned in Newfoundland, was carrying freight from Halifax and different places in Newfoundland during the war. On one trip, when leaving Halifax with a load of high-test gas, she disappeared. It seems the ship blew up after a coal fire was lit.

On a return trip from St. Pierre Bank, the *Marjorie and Dorothy* came across a number of barrels containing gas assumed to have been aboard the *Margaret K. Smith*. They put out the dories and picked up some forty-eight barrels and also salvaged part of the ill-fated vessel's name plaque. When they came into Halifax, they reported their findings to Imperial Oil, who came to collect the barrels. The crew received compensation at the rate of two dollars a barrel. However, the crew held one barrel back for the cleaning of engine parts during winter refit in Lunenburg.

At refit time, the *Marjorie and Dorothy*'s mate had filled a sawed-off drum with the salvaged high-test gas, and the drum was positioned near a stove burning with a hard coal fire. While cleaning a part, the mate accidently dropped it in the barrel, causing a splash that reached the blazing stove. Inevitably there was an explosion. The mate was badly burned and the cabin sustained heavy damage.

Firemen and crew joined forces to fight the encroaching flames. They urgently needed to remove a five-gallon keg of gun powder that was kept to load the swivel cannon and stored in a cupboard behind the captain's bunk. The firefighters cut a hole in the roof of the cabin house and dropped a hose down. Then they flooded the cabin and managed to remove the powder keg safely. The skipper would later say, "I'm some glad they got that out before, because that would have blew the right side out of her and probably killed half was aboard there yet." Thanks to the combined efforts of firemen and crew, the vessel was saved. At some point a crew member had taken some of the high-test gas home to burn in his car. As Matthew says, "It burned her up you!"

One dirty day on Western Bank, when it was "actually not fit to be in a dory," Matt and Owen Grandy had their dory up on the windward end. They had set the middle thwart seat up on its edge to make more room for their catch. They were keeping a watchful eye on the water around them yet Matthew says, "Where this sea come from we don't know. He topped up you and he come right in and cleaned the middle place right out."

In fact, the waves had taken almost everything out of the dory. There was so much water aboard they had to use a trawl tub to bail her out. They managed to retrieve some of the gear, especially the paddles, but Matt told his dorymate, "Owen, Mossman didn't drown us this time and he's never getting a chance to drown me again. When I get in, this is it." Owen chimed in, "That goes for me too."

Although Matt felt Captain Mossman was a "good man" and was satisfied with him overall, that incident and the rough sea was one of the closest calls he ever had and it could have been all over for him and Owen. Despite his words, however, Matt went back to sea and eventually became a captain. Owen Grady would also go on to become a captain.

## Special Hazards of
## Dory and Winter Fishing

There were hard days in the dories in the wintertime. Even the fish would be frozen, their eyes turned white from the cold. That made cleaning the fish a much slower process, and the ones on top of a pile would be particularly hard.

Matthew remembers some yarns Captain Jim Goslin told him from his salt fishing days when they would be up around Rose Blanche fishing for cod. Jim was dorymate with one of the Hollett brothers. He would take the sounding lead with him in the dory in the morning and would guide the dories where to set. Sometimes it would be mid-afternoon before they would see the vessel, in winter weather no less.

Jim said one time they were out all week fishing in pretty good weather and when they came in on Saturday they had a deckload of frozen fish. They hauled out some dories, filled them full of water and thawed the fish before splitting them. Jim's dorymate would claim that he never did seem him sleep.

Once a vessel was returning with a lean trip of fish. Someone remarked to Jim they must have had a Jonah, a bad luck spirit aboard. Captain Goslin retorted he knew who the Jonah was. He told the fellow, "Your Jonah sleeps in the skipper's bunk." The loyal crewman took exception to this remark and was about to get physical with Jim Goslin when the Jonah skipper himself intervened, having seen the humour in the comment.

Winter fishing could be even more hazardous if you were with a skipper who was less than caring. Matthew knows of one vessel that lost three dories one winter and of another that lost two dories in one day. Rumour had it one of the crew had told the captain, while they were securing the dories on deck at the end of the day, "Skipper, there's dories not on board." The captain allegedly had responded, "That's nothing. They've only been gone since eight o'clock this morning."

On one vessel Matt had sailed on, the captain went looking for a man who was unaccounted for at baiting time. He found him lying in his bunk with a badly injured hand. The skipper said to him, "What's wrong with you? Your old man was tough. What are you made of?"

One icy April morning on another vessel fishing around Sable Island, another skipper sought out a sick man who had remained in his bunk down forward. The captain hollered to him, "Only dead men stays lying down there!"

While Matt was with a vessel out of Liverpool, one winter day when his own ship was staying in port, he and the crew watched another vessel go out. They noticed it returning around eleven o'clock the same day and it was not long before the news got around that two of their crewmen had gone missing.

Dories were known to upset, like the one Matt's father-in-law was in when it rolled over alongside its vessel. In a separate incident, a ship ran down a dory and the two dorymen went right under the vessel. Fortunately, they were saved.

It was not unheard of for fishermen who went astray to row or sail ashore. One Newfoundland vessel, anchored on Banquereau, had two men go astray. After twenty-four hours of searching and waiting for the missing dories, the ship went into Burin. On arrival the captain was passed a message that his crewmen had landed at Cape Lahune; they had rowed and sailed approximately two hundred miles in their dory. Similarly, when the *Astrid W.* was lost off Louisbourg, some men made it ashore in dories.

## Chapter 5

## Preparing To Take Command

### Learning Navigation:
### The Isabel F. Spindler

When Matt went with Captain Willet Spindler on the *Isabel F. Spindler*, he asked permission to bring an old sextant, a half-quadrant, and a navigation chart on board. When the skipper looked at the instrument he said, "Dump it overboard – that's no good." Then he asked Matt, "Do you want to learn navigation?"

Having received a positive response, he took Matt down to the cabin where he retrieved a beautiful brass sextant from the chest. He placed it on the table and removed the cover. "Now," he said, gesturing with his fingers pointing down, "when you take it out you take it like this and you put it back the same way because if you don't, you won't have it."

They went up on deck and the captain went through the steps required to take a sight. Matt remembers it was quite a while before he got the hang of it. When he did, the skipper produced the almanac and everything else that was required to do the calculations.

For what seemed like a long time, Matt kept practis-ing getting the bearings and marking them on his chart. He

The crew of the *Isabel F. Spindler*. Matt is standing, second from the left.

would show them to the captain who at first said nothing; he would not confirm whether they were right or wrong. In time he seemed to take more interest and every now and then he would ask Matt, "Where have you got her today?"

He would never say yea or nay to Matt's figures, even the day on St. Pierre Bank when he called it, just as the old-timers did, "twenty on the line." Another time on Banquereau Matt suspects the skipper, who was a good navigator, was having difficulty getting situated where he needed to be. He asked his pupil to take the sight, but again, would not confirm which one had been more accurate.

On a trip home Matt was on watch off St. Pierre Bank when he saw someone firing flares. The captain told Matt to change course for him. The distress signals were coming from Captain Johnny Beck, who had broken down around Quero and was requesting that Captain Spindler call for a towboat.

The towboat operators had requested the position of the vessel, so the skipper told his understudy, "Mitchell, you go down and get the sextant and take a sight."

Matt, who had been dressing fish, took off his rubber clothes, threw them on the cabin house and did as he was told. He had everything figured out and written down before he went back up to give the captain the readings. Matt overheard the skipper giving the towboat their exact position: it was just as he had calculated. Finally, Matt came to the conclusion that if the captain was not questioning his readings, then they must be accurate.

The *Isabel F. Spindler* would be the last sailing fishing vessel Matt would work on. When he left he sold his chart to Captain Spindler for ninety cents. Although the skipper tried to give him a dollar for it, his apprentice insisted on giving him the ten cents back. Matt's dorymate, Cecil Lace, left the *Isabel F. Spindler* at the same time.

## From Dories to Trawlers:
## The Cape North

Both Matt and Cecil were anxious to get a chance on the *Cape North*, a new trawler they had heard was looking for men from time to time. So one day in 1947 Matt went down to the docks and Captain Tom Pittman happened to be standing on the bridge of the *Cape North*. He called to Matt, "Laddie, are you looking for a chance?"

Matt answered, "Yes, I would like to have a chance." The captain called back, "Okay, then there is one here for you." Matt told him, "My clothes are in Halifax and we haven't got the fish out yet." The skipper replied, "It don't make no difference. We're not going until Monday anyway. So you go in tomorrow and take your fish out."

Matthew recollects, "I half knew him and he half knew me. I think I did one time ask him if I could get a chance." Captain Pittman had recently taken command of the *Cape North* following the passing of Captain Napean Crouse.

Side trawlers had a dramatic effect on harvesting the riches of the sea.

Fishing from trawlers was altogether a different world and Matt found it a big change. He confided to the captain that he did not know what to do aboard. The skipper's reply was, "If you don't know how to shoot and haul in six hours, you'll never learn it."

Matt also felt he knew little about mending nets but the mate and even the skipper would help those anxious to learn that skill. Matthew recalls, "Mostly a bunch of us in our watch we would get in underneath the bow and a fella who would know how to do it he learned us. We practised at it until we learned how to do it."

There were other aspects of dragging that had to be learned, like how to deal with "tanglefoot" or "cancer" as they used to call it. These were spiderweb-like clusters of seaweed that would get into the nets and tear them up.

"That was something to get out too," Matthew declares. "I seen it already when the ground cable come up before you seen the net. You would have to have the fire axe. That would be all around the warps [a three-quarter-inch cable] so big as a pork barrel. You had to cut it out before you could get into the net."

They used cowhides and buffalo hides to keep the cod end from chafing through. The cowhides were sometimes coated with manure, "old gurry" they used to call it while the buffalo hides were huge, which made them heavy and hard to handle. Vigilance and improvisation were required.

It was not long after Matt had joined the *Cape North* that they went into Sydney to seek refuge from a hurricane that was coming down the coast. They planned to take the fish out in North Sydney but before they could finish the task, increasing wind velocity drove them to South Sydney, where they tied up to a stronger pier.

The *Cape North* was a new vessel and had recently been in refit: she was gleaming from every one of her shiny white parts. While tied up in South Sydney, she was near an old coal carrier that was being loaded. Every time a carload of coal was dumped, the dust blew onto everything in proximity. Aboard the *Cape North*, the coal dust seeped into everything, even places like lockers and other enclosures. The next morning the winds had subsided so they returned to North Sydney to finish taking the fish out. Meanwhile, Matt had spent the night with relatives in North Sydney. When he returned to the ship the next morning, he did not recognize her – everything that had been white was now black.

The *Cape North* was landing fish in many places, which was partly due to its owner, National Sea, having cold storage facilities in a number of locations. One time when the *Cape North* was disabled due to a broken high-pressure fuel pump, they were towed into Matt's hometown of Burin. This was an unexpected detour that for Matt meant he would be returning to his native village for the first time since leaving home some twenty years ago. However, in an ironic twist of fate, his parents had left on a trip to Lunenburg that very morning. When Matt returned to port in Lunenburg, they would go on to have a memorable visit after all.

The draggers went into refit once a year. Matthew remembers, "You would strip her when you'd leave to come in off of your last trip; you'd cut the net off and have everything ready. When you went on the slip you done everything – the crew would clean her up, scrubbed her from top to bottom. Down in the hold you used caustic soda. How many times did I come up, you wouldn't know what you had the measles where your face would be burned where the water splashed. We were a gang of men down there scrubbing that out with those bloody old birch brooms and that splashing around. Today you would be hung if you done that. There was no payment for that – it was all free labour."

The crew would be paid when they undertook painting jobs on the ship. The cook on the *Cape North*, Dougie Whynacht, once offered to paint the boards from the fish pens. There were seventeen hundred pen boards and each board was three feet long by six inches wide. Dougie loaded them on a truck and took them home to paint, then returned them to the ship.

While Matt started on the *Cape North* as deckhand, he would go on to be bosun, then mate, until Captain Pittman retired. Following Captain Pittman's retirement in April 1956, Matt accepted command of the *Cape North*.

## CAPTAIN MITCHELL AT THE HELM:
## THE CAPE NORTH

The challenges facing the captain of a fishing boat were endless. As far as fish went, the quality of the catch could be as weighty as quantity. For instance, when fishing for flounder, you could take in a trip with a significant percentage of "jelly flounder." For reasons not fully understood at the time, a portion of the catch would spoil sooner than the rest, causing the fish's flesh to take on a jelly-like consistency, making it unsuitable for choice markets. Since this condition usually prevailed during the summer months, it was generally believed that sole dependence on ice for refrigeration might combine with warmer water temperatures to accelerate spoilage.

On one trip Captain Mitchell was in the *Cape North* and Captain Cecil Garland was in the *Cape Bonnie*. They went down over the eastern edge of the Grand Banks and struck a sizeable bunch of flounder. Matthew recollects, "Look here, they were the biggest kind you. I used to say to Cecil when we were catching them, we'll be hung this time. When we get in the whole works of this will be jelly." Cecil agreed but felt they should catch them anyway. After they filled the two boats, the *Cape Bonnie* went into Halifax and the *Cape North* into Lunenburg.

Captain Mitchell came down to the dock in the morning after some of the fish had been taken out. He asked the foreman what the fish were like. The foreman answered, "Not bad at all." As a matter of fact, when the fish were all out, the jelly flounder accounted for only two to three percent. Matt called Cecil and asked, "How did you make out with the flounder?" Cecil replied, "Wonderful. It was only five percent. We're going down to see if we can get another one."

Matthew reflects, "That was a godsend in the summertime because the fish used to be pretty scarce then. When we were going for flounder, that saved your neck when you used to get them."

Matt's several years of experience aboard the *Cape North* before becoming its captain had taught him that side trawlers could be particularly challenging in rough weather. Because you had to haul your gear over the side, Matthew says, "If it was rough weather there was always a chance that she could ship a sea and probably clean the deck off." Ice buildup on deck was a recurring problem as they did a lot of fishing around the Gulf of St. Lawrence, northern Newfoundland and the Grand Banks.

Captain Mitchell's worst day on the *Cape North* and one of the saddest in his life was the night a man was killed aboard. They had been fishing on what was a fine night. Matt had turned in, around midnight as usual, when he heard a man call his name. The next thing he knew there was a fellow in his cabin shaking him and shouting, "We've got a man killed!" Matthew still shivers at the memory of waking up to those words.

The unfortunate man had been using a long bar to guide the warp on the drum winch; draggers were not equipped with automatic guide-on gear. When the shackle link came up it caught the bar, which went back and struck him under the ear. It appears he was killed instantly. He fell on the warp and his body made three or four turns on the drum.

Matthew remembers, "That was one of the hardest things. I looked at him and I couldn't stay there. Grover Watson was there and I told him I didn't think I could get that man off there. Grover said to me, 'Skipper, you stay up in the wheel-house and I'll get somebody to help me.' Of course I went down when they had gotten the body off. It was terrible to look at. There was nobody could have survived that. Lloyd Feener was a fine man from Lunenburg." RCMP officers came aboard to conduct an investigation and Dr. Saunders made out his coroner's report. The death was ruled accidental.

Of the many adventures Captain Mitchell would experience aboard the *Cape North*, some could only be described as being in the realm of the unexplained. On one trip they were down to Cape St. Mary's and the fishing was good. They had a deck full of fish and were coming around to shoot the gear away again when they saw two ships coming.

Jack Rowlands was mate and the captain asked him, "On the radar, how close are they?" The mate answered, "There's nothing on the radar." Matthew says, "Me and him got into a half a row and I said to him, the name of God Almighty, you can't see that on the radar?"

The skipper went to see for himself and sure enough there was nothing on the radar. Yet there were two ships there, large as life, coming down side by side. They let the dragger come around and stopped. Matthew says, "Look here, we watched and they come so close: two big sailing ships. Then all of a sudden, they disappeared, just like that, and there was nothing there! After that different people told me that they seen them, whatever it was."

Another episode of the unexplained had to do with a ghost ship, the *Young Teazer*, people would see coming in and out of Lunenburg on summer nights. This schooner-rigged vessel had exploded in the waters of Mahone Bay while being pursued by five British navy vessels in 1813, during the war between America and Britain. A young American officer on board had been part of previous raids against the British. He opted to set fire to the munitions rather than be captured and sent to the gallows. All but eight hands on board the *Young Teazer* were lost, allegedly including the culprit. Matt had never witnessed this apparition. However, one time going out of Lunenburg on the *Cape North*, they got to the buoy and put the ship on course.

The captain was back in his cabin changing his clothes. He heard somebody holler, "There's a ship right ahead!" The skipper went out and saw a full-rigged ship. Matthew says "The name of God I didn't know what to make of it. She was right in our path but she was a little ways away. All of a sudden we were getting up close enough to pull away from her. She was all lit up you, and the lights went out right from the top right to the water. Then there was nothing there."

Heavy seas batter a trawler.

Decks awash aboard a trawler.

Of course, there was much chatter on board as to what they had seen, whether it was the *Young Teazer* or something else. Then the very next fall, on the same date at the same time of night, again the *Cape North* was going out of Lunenburg. Someone called to the captain that there was a ship ahead and when Matt came out, there she was again. Matt told his crewman to call for Charlie Miller, who was down having a cup of tea. The skipper asked him, "Uncle Charlie, what do you make of that?" Charlie answered, "That's the *Teazer*. I seen her many's a time in my time going in and out of here, always with an easterly coming up." Sure enough, that was a beautiful night but, as Matthew recalls, "It was making up from the east. She disappeared the same time as the first time we seen it. The lights went out from the top and come right down."

Altogether, Matt would serve on the *Cape North* some nineteen years, ten of them as captain. Following the *Cape North*, he was offered command of the Cape Norman.

## THE CAPE NORMAN

While the *Cape North* had been a wooden side trawler, the *Cape Norman* was a steel trawler, which was considered a more modern ship. Captain Mitchell would only be with the *Cape Norman* a year or so.

Something peculiar happened one time they were fishing on Georges Bank. There was a northwest wind blowing and it was cold. The crew was stripping the ice off the boat when the mate accidently knocked the bell overboard; it had been frozen in the ice. Some twenty years later, Matt's son David was fishing on the *Freedom 99* with Captain Morash in command. While hauling in scallops, they discovered the *Cape Norman*'s bell in the pile. Matthew says, "There was no way to try to find the bell over there when it fell into forty-odd fathom of water. But they were scalloping, see, and dragging everything up through mud, rock and everything." Matthew still shakes his head at the fact that, of all the deckhands who were hauling nets that day, it was his son who had pulled up the bell.

## THE CAPE PICTOU

In the mid-1960s, stern trawlers were coming on stream. Captain Anthony Kelly got command of the *Cape Pictou* when it was first launched. He kept it until he moved back to Newfoundland in the late 1960s, following which it was offered to Captain Mitchell.

The stern trawler, or dragger, did not present the same dangers as the side trawler in rough weather and was more efficient. In the stern trawler, everything came up a ramp over the stern. Thirty or forty minutes from the time you started to haul, the gear was in the water again and everybody was below deck dressing fish. On the side trawlers, like the *Cape North* and the *Cape Norman*, the fish was dressed on deck. Matthew says of the *Cape Pictou*, "She was quite a nice boat. In fact, she was one of the best of that type of dragger. She was a good sea boat and her superstructure wasn't so high as on some of the rest."

Still, whether it be in a side dragger or a stern dragger, fishing remained a challenge. Matthew remembers when the *Cape Pictou* and the *Cape Scotia*, with Captain Paul George, were up in the Gulf of St. Lawrence around St. Paul's. The codfish there proved to be too small so they left and went north to Cape George in Newfoundland. Matthew recalls, "We shot away and we were three days and a half until we swung her off. Not a man seen the bunk, except the chief engineer, in all that time."

The last set they made they hauled 25,000 to 30,000 codfish. They headed out and everyone except the chief engineer turned in for six hours of sleep. Matthew says, "Then we got out and dressed the fish and of course, cleaned everything up. Some of them trips was pretty hard."

Another time the *Cape Pictou* was coming out of the St. Lawrence. There had been a lot of fish up there and the boat was pretty full. It had been a fine day with no wind, but just as they got the deck cleaned off the weather changed suddenly.

"She pitched a living storm: nor'west and snow and frost, the name of God how cold did it get!" Matthew recalls. "Two

Ice build-up was a serious hazard, making a ship top-heavy and difficult to manage.

or three hours from that and we didn't know what to do with her: that's how quick they iced up. We were off Cape Anquille there and we got out so far as Cape Ray and by gollies, I'll tell you there was ice on her then and she was loaded. She was deep in the water and you could fair see her settling away, sinking down."

They had a struggle to keep the ice off her and they had to go slow and keep cutting in, head to the wind. Eventually, they spotted a field of ice and shoved her in there as far as they could go, stopped and cleaned her up. When they got out of the ice they were able to go full speed ahead. The hurricane-force winds were not letting up. They stopped again off Ingonish, then around Scatterie, off Louisbourg and at White Head off Canso, to pound ice. The ice had to be cleaned off every few hours.

On one trip in the Gulf of St. Lawrence, pressure from ice around the rudder interfered with the ship's hydraulic system. All the pipes burst, rendering the steering inoperable. Fortunately, they were able to jury-rig a rudder to make the trip home.

Crewmen work to clear the ice.

A sad memory for Captain Mitchell from his days on the *Cape Pictou* was the death of Walter (Teddy) Corkum. Teddy was getting along in years, so he only used to go fishing in the spring. The first day out that spring, the mate came up and told the captain that Teddy was not feeling well. The skipper went down and asked him, "Do you want to go in? Because Burgess will be going in." Captain Forbes Burgess was in the *Cape Bauld* and they took Teddy to hospital, where he succumbed to a heart attack. Teddy Corkum had been one of the men saved when the *Flora Alberta* collided with the steamer *Fanad Head* in April 1943. Twenty-one men were lost in that tragic accident.

After some nine years on the *Pictou*, Captain Mitchell was offered command of the *Cape Bauld* following the passing of Captain Burgess.

## THE CAPE BAULD

Captain Mitchell's last command was the *Cape Bauld*. Hull-wise, she was the same as the *Cape Pictou*. However, Matthew says, "I don't think she was so good a sea boat because she had a bigger house onto her, more of a superstructure, but she was still a good boat."

## COOKS AT SEA

Matt saw his share of cooks in the course of his long fishing career. He particularly has good memories of meals prepared by Willoughby Mills, Walton Parks, Clary Allen, Seymour Tanner and Lawrence Tanner. "There was a lot of good cooks," Matthew recollects, "but then there was a lot that wasn't too hot. In some of them old vessels, sometimes I don't know why we weren't all poisoned. When you would have a meal and the first table would have eaten, the cook would take a mug if there was some tea left into it, and he would go from one to the other. That is the way he would rinse them out, he would go all around the table and then throw that away. We used to have those mugs hung up. There was twenty-odd men and there was six mugs hanging. Everyone was drinking out of that. When you had yours finished, you just dumped what was left over into the slop bucket, rolled it around your sleeve, and hung it up for the next fella. But some cooks were so clean as a new pin. Everything had to be just so and you had to be just so or they let you know."

## RETIRING TO A NEW OCCUPATION

In 1977 it came time for Captain Mitchell to relinquish command of fishing boats. He had been going to sea for nearly fifty years and it was time to retire. But his withdrawal from the sea would not mean retirement in the traditional sense. He was soon to embrace a new occupation rooted in the sea.

# Chapter 6

# Shore Captain
# at the Fisheries Museum

## Fisheries Museum of the Atlantic

In spite of spending the majority of his time at sea, Matt managed to actively participate in key organizations of his adopted town. He was a member of the Lunenburg Board of Trade for a number of years and served on the Board of Directors of the Fisheries Museum.

Even before being recruited to serve as its shore captain, Matt took a hands-on approach to helping build the museum's collection. The *Cape North* was donated to the museum in January 1972, and Captain Mitchell took on fitting out the captain's cabin for the ship's display of what had been his first trawler command. This entailed providing the mattress, blanket and pillowcase, the weatherglass, charts and other navigation artifacts. Pending his retirement from his sea-going career, Matt delegated the maintenance of the captain's cabin contents to Captain Albert Crouse. The items had to be gathered up in the fall, the linens washed, and everything returned to the display vessel the following spring.

The *Theresa E. Connor* was donated in 1966 and is considered to be the flagship of the museum. She was the last of the salt bank schooners to operate from Lunenburg. The *Theresa E. Connor* belongs to the class of "auxiliary" schooners in that she is fitted with an engine.

In 1977, the year Matt relinquished command of the *Cape Bauld* to resume his life on land, he received a visit at Christmas time from John Meisner, Sr. and Ainsley Fralick, board members at the Fisheries Museum. Captain Albert Crouse was retiring as shore captain of the museum and the two men had come to offer Captain Mitchell the position.

The shore captain's responsibilities included maintenance of everything aboard the three display vessels, being at that time the *Cape North*, the *Theresa E. Connor*, and the rum-runner *Reo II*, donated in time for the 1971 season. The up-keep of any items that might be placed on the wharf were also the domain of the shore captain. The public aspect of his role was to greet visitors who came aboard these boats and answer any questions they might have.

## SHORE CAPTAIN MITCHELL

When Shore Captain Mitchell first went to work, there was no dock that belonged to the museum. All three display vessels were tied up at the goodwill of the merchants bordering the waterfront. When National Sea moved out to Battery Point, the museum vessels could be tied up on site. However, these facilities were in shabby condition and the wharves were literally falling down. The buildings were old and derelict and in the early stages the public would be brought aboard on planks of plywood, as Matthew says, "Like you would herd cattle." There was a shack-like structure where tickets and souvenirs were sold and there was only one washroom facility.

However, the rundown facilities were balanced by the congenial company. Matthew reminisces, "We had great fellas to work with. First when I come, there was Russell Tanner and Lawrence Tanner, Gibby Tanner and myself. After that I worked with a lot of other good fellas: Fred Moore and Everett Tanner, George Dominix, Jobe Fry, Murray Lohnes,

Ross Knickle, Percy Morash, Cyril Tanner, carpenter Dennis Mader, boat builders Eddie Mosher and Wayne Davison, Rosie Tanner and a number of others."

Then the Town of Lunenburg purchased the property from National Sea and renovations progressed piece by piece. Ainsley Fralick, president of the board, was contacting a lot of people for support and as a result of his negotiations, federal government money was granted to rebuild the wharves. Two of the buildings were beyond salvaging and had to be torn down. Matt was involved in tearing down one of those buildings, a large structure occupying the length of the dock where *Bluenose II* ties up today.

The work began after the museum closed in the fall. They took down a section each day and would clean up the good wood and haul the unuseable wood away. They saved all the lumber that could be recycled; in fact, the steps in the current museum came from that old building. While the docks were being built, the expansion of the buildings continued. The former electrical shop in the National Sea plant became the gift shop and also home of the first aquarium.

As with any restoration work, there were setbacks. Ainsley had requested the workers who were restoring what had been the old ice house to "stake" the planks onto the old mud floor. This way they could be laid in such a way that air would circulate through them. After removing tons of lumber, fish boxes and other sundry, they proceeded to stake the heavy rough lumber on the old mud floor. One morning they returned to the site to find the lumber being hauled away. Matthew recounts, "Here was the gang from National taking it all out after we worked there for two weeks staking it. So we never got the good of that!" Next they cleaned out the old machine shop, which was filled with shafts and assorted parts.

Then it was time to collect furnishings and artifacts for the museum. Again the small group of museum workers rose to the task and systematically sifted through the contents of buildings belonging to nearly every business on the waterfront, sorting the items and picking up what could be used at the museum. There were many contributions from the residents of Lunenburg, notably principal patron Captain Angus Tanner.

"In them days I used to be around with Captain Angus Tanner quite a lot," Matthew recollects. "Angus was bringing in artifacts – he was picking up trawl gear and hook sets, old chests, you name it. I worked with Angus quite a bit at that, looking after the stuff for him. We had it recorded one time – it seems to me like seventeen hundred pieces that he had collected. The last time I was out to his house we went out and filled some trawl tubs with things for the museum. We brought loads of artifacts from Riverport and even over to Bush Island and a lot of different places."

Initially, the gift shop had been housed in an old shack in the parking area. The admission tickets were also sold from there and Virginia Hebb was the seasonal employee in charge of the venture. When the gift shop was moved to the main building, Ruby Whynacht was asked to manage it, assisted by Thelma Allen. The gift shop was a significant source of revenue for the museum. It was natural for visitors to want to acquire something tangible that would remind them of their memorable visit to the Fisheries Museum of the Atlantic. When Ruby retired in October 1996, she and Captain Mitchell held the longest service records at the museum. Ruby was succeeded by Ann Tanner, who remains the gift shop's manager to this day.

In the early 1970s, it was recognized that a more professional approach was required in hiring and utilizing tour guides. Barbara Spindler organized a group tour program for schools and other potential users.

After a few years of the small group's efforts, the museum was taking shape. They had a good sound wharf to tie the vessels to. They now had the *Theresa E. Connor*, the *Cape North* and the *Reo II* on display and they had to be fitted out every spring. The employees would come in the first of April for opening the first of May.

"All three vessels had to be scrubbed down on the slip and painted," Matthew recollects. "Then the galley would be set and everything. You had to have good weather to be finished in a month in time for opening. In the *Theresa E. Connor*, the hold would be fitted, just the same as if you wanted to go fishing. Everything was aboard her and everything was in place. Many's the hours that we spent in the evening after everybody was gone, me and Wilf Eisnor – after supper to afore we opened to put all the exhibits up. We had to have it done before opening: that was one of John and Ainsley's mottoes.

"At different times some of the board members would come down and tell us we'd never be ready this year because we only had a few days left, but we always got her ready. They would come when we had it done, sit with us at the table down below and tell us how beautiful everything looked and what a good job we done onto it."

During the winter months Captain Mitchell would be the sole employee, except for Annette Hayward, the secretary, who looked after all office matters including payroll. Carpenters would be brought in as required, which of course they were while the restoration and expansion of the buildings was going on. In those days Matt would assist them. He remembers one of them would not let him drive nails, because, he said, "You'll bruise the wood." Matthew recalls, "If there was anything to be painted up I used to paint it. One winter I had everything painted up myself. There was always something to do. There was hardly a day that I wasn't gone somewhere for something."

When bad weather threatened, Matt would do whatever it took to prevent the boats from breaking away from the docks. He says, "When I first came ashore I was down here the whole night because the old wharves, they were scared she [*Theresa E. Connor*] would break away from the dock. One night in particular Wilf Eisnor he helped me and I had to call my son David out to come down to help me get lines out to hold her."

Matt tells of one time being over to Atlantic Ship with president John Meisner when a sou'eastern had been blowing all night. He was helping to secure the scallop draggers, but one had still managed to break loose and was adrift in the harbour where there was a big swell.

"I seen this thing was dragging and there still was a nice puff of wind," Matthew recollects. "She was coming in and she was coming right for the *Theresa*. I didn't know what to do. We had a huge tire, we had a strap on it; we used to use it for putting on the edge of the dock for something to bump up against."

Matt spotted Murray Gurney in the parking lot. Murray called out, "She's going to come in and hit the *Theresa*."

Matt hollered back, "Murray, come and give me a lift." Together they wrestled the old tire down and put it on the *Theresa*'s quarter. "By gollies, that's right where she hit up against that – she didn't do any damage to her. It would have been all over if it wasn't for that big rubber tire," Matthew remarks.

When the museum first opened, the working hours were loosely structured. It seemed to Matt that he and Lawrence Tanner, his co-worker, were passing one another every couple of hours on the road. Matthew recalls, "You would be down there for three or four hours, then you would be going home for dinner and the other fella would be coming in. We were open until eight o'clock in the evenings at that time in summertime. I enjoyed it in the evening. Many's the evening we would lock up the building at eight o'clock but we'd have a bunch down forward aboard the *Cape North* or the *Theresa*. Me and Lawrence and those fellows, we would sit down and answer questions probably for a couple of hours after closing."

In the course of developing the museum, various displays and exhibits were moved, enhanced or removed, according to the wishes of the Museum Society. A link was built to connect the two buildings. Parks Canada took over an upstairs room. The aquarium moved over into what used to be the ice house. Local fishermen would cooperate in stocking the aquarium – every morning at opening time either Russell Tanner, Walter Feener or Bob Tanner would bring fresh fish. The upstairs featured the sail loft, rum-running exhibit and the theatre.

Currently, the small boats are displayed in what used to be a coal shed. The carpenter shop and the dory shop are big attractions and the ships tied to the dock are also a major draw with visitors. Matthew says, "They think it is wonderful even to get aboard a boat, let alone go through it. They get the feeling of it, especially if they're moving a little. People will ask if they're floating or exclaim that the boat is moving."

In his experience Matthew feels what captured visitors' interest the most was having the opportunity to gather around him or one of his fishing comrades to hear them talk about what it was like during their fishing days. There seemed to him to be a particular fascination for the dory fishing days. As well, there is a lot of curiosity about the *Bluenose*, why it is famous and why it is on the Canadian dime. Matthew says, "If you can talk on the *Bluenose* and the salt fishing it is no problem – you can talk all day. They like to say they get it from the horse's mouth, from the people that went through it."

Disasters at sea also spark a lot of interest as usually visitors have stopped by the Memorial monument before going into the museum. People tend to think because there are long lists of names like Tanner or Whynacht, they must have been all members of one family. "I talked to a lot of people and I never talked to one that ever got tired of listening to those yarns," Matthew affirms. "Never one that ever turned away, sometimes nearly missing their tour bus departure." Visitors loved to take pictures of Captain Mitchell in the dory and of themselves in there with him.

Matthew regrets the removal of the salt fish display. "We had a beautiful display," he reminisces. "We had codfish, salt cod, salt hake, salt pollock, salt herring, pickled herring and even squid, capelin and Digby chicks." Although he feels the addition of a touch tank was a good thing, particularly for visiting children, he would have preferred to see the salt fishing display moved to the fish store area rather than displaced altogether.

Ironically, the worst day of Matt's association with fishing and the sea was spent on shore while he was employed with the museum. It was the day the *Margaret Jane* and the *Cape Beaver* collided off Lunenburg Harbour. Captain Mitchell was off that day but heard the news almost right after it happened, around eleven o'clock in the morning.

The *Margaret Jane* had come in to land a man and was not out long before she was run down. The accident was made all the more traumatic for the Mitchell family because son David was on board. Matt went down to the ship company where they confirmed the collision and reported that there was loss of life. It would be several hours before the names of the men lost would become known. Olive had to be sedated; the doctor came to the house and stayed with her while they waited. Hundreds of people in Lunenburg and Newfoundland were going through the same anguish – waiting, hoping, praying.

Finally, Matthew recounts, "Six o'clock some time Winnie Mitchell, Billy's wife, she come tearing in the door saying she had seen them taking David off of her. Then we knew there was hopes then." A couple more long hours went by before they received the news that David was all right.

Since his retirement from the Fisheries Museum, Captain Mitchell continues to receive cards and letters from all over the world from visitors to the museum who claim it was the highlight of their trip to Nova Scotia. From his standpoint, Matthew enjoyed entertaining the visitors. He also met many dignitaries, including Governor General Ed Schreyer and Mrs. Schreyer, Madame Desmarais, Hillary Rodham Clinton, and ministers from the Trinidad government, to name but a few.

## Ambassador Mitchell

In the course of his employment with the museum, Captain Mitchell had the opportunity to travel as representative of the Fisheries Museum of the Atlantic.

He hosted a dory display in Ottawa in 1986 for the week celebrating Canada Day. The first day he was told that 42,000 visitors had passed through Victoria Island on the Rideau Canal, where the exhibits were on display. Matthew is sure three-quarters of those people stopped by his dory because by the end of the afternoon he was so hoarse he could hardly talk. During the exhibition he distributed hundreds of pins of Nova Scotia, the *Bluenose*, and the fisherman's symbol. He could not replace them on the dory thwart fast enough.

On the second day of the exhibition, a windy rainstorm had passed through during the night, blowing over some of the exhibit tents. Captain Mitchell's dory exhibit was too long to fit under a tent and so had been open to the elements. Inside the dory there was a model of the *Bluenose* made by Captain Calvin Silver. The wind had turned it bottom up.

As Matthew says, "The spars and everything was out of her and when I came in and seen that in the morning I told myself that boat was gone. But a fella by the name of Hines, right there by me in the Newfoundland tent, he was a model boat builder. When I told him I was shot, he said not to worry – he would take the model and fix it so it would be as good as new. Sure enough, the next morning you could never tell that she was ever bottom up."

Matthew says there was not much time for sightseeing during that week but in the evening the exhibitors would go out for dinner. During the day Matt would be dressed in his fishing clothes with heavy pants, sweater, shirt and leather boots. In the evening his companions insisted he keep the leather boots on as these proved irresistible for people to come over and feel for what they were made of. On the last night a reception was held in the West Block of the Parliament Buildings for all the exhibitors. Matthew says that was the one time he had a dance on Parliament Hill.

Captain Mitchell was also invited to join the Sea Sell expedition. This was a tourism venture whereby several town and business representatives from the South Shore of Nova Scotia boarded the *Scotia Prince* bound for Boston, Baltimore and Philadelphia. Their mission was to promote the region. In the various ports, people would come aboard to view the exhibits.

Matthew recalls, "In Boston we had hundreds of people an hour aboard, but the biggest crowd we had was in Baltimore. We were there two days." One visitor in Baltimore asked Captain Mitchell, "Where is Lunenburg? I never heard tell of that before." Matthew rejoined swiftly, "You haven't got very many Canadian hundred dollar bills." The fellow retorted, rather sharply, "How do you know what I got?" Matthew replied, "If you did you would know where Lunenburg is."

The fellow's wife, who had been engaged in conversation with Matthew prior to the interruption, laughed and told her husband, "You asked for that one."

Captain Mitchell was also involved in provincial tours. Teaming up with the museum curator and the historian, he featured exhibits at the World Trade and Convention Centre in Halifax and at schools around the province.

While in the museum's employ, Captain Mitchell appeared in two commercials for the Bank of Nova Scotia. One was set in Indian Harbour and involved casting a large net, meant to symbolize the globe, to signal the presence of Scotiabank branches around the world.

Even on his personal time, Matthew would promote the Fisheries Museum. On vacation he would carry brochures and pins and hand them out or leave them in motels and hotels where he was staying, as far away as Hawaii. He cannot say for certain, but to his knowledge, prior to his trip to Hawaii the museum had not recorded visitors from that part of the world. Yet in later years, tourists from Hawaii made the Fisheries Museum one of their stops in Nova Scotia.

## Bidding the Museum Farewell

At the age of ninety years, it came time for Captain Mitchell to take his official leave from the Fisheries Museum in 2007. In his thirty years of tenure as shore captain, he served under five board presidents and five museum managers. But the invisible hawser that linked the museum to Matthew's house, less than a block away, would not be severed. At every opportunity, he and his daughter Joan, an interpreter at the museum for several years, make their former place of employment a must stop on their neighbourhood strolls.

# Epilogue

# Afterword
# from the Mitchell Children

Fishing families live with the timeworn reality of a husband or father being away at sea most of the time. The elder Mitchell children, Joan and Sherman, grew up while their father fished on sailing vessels. Then the voyages were long and the shore leaves short. Susan and David, eleven to nineteen years younger, were raised in a more modern fishery, mainly while their father was a ship captain. Though his absences were still frequent, the trips were usually shorter and Dad would be home while the ship he skippered was in refit.

"Growing up it was Mom that made us a family since she was always there, although there was no doubt in my mind Dad was the real head of the family. The times Dad spent at home were so short. He might be there when I came home from school, but he would be gone when I got up the next morning. Christmas, though, was made even more exciting because we expected Dad home. I remember him carrying me on his shoulders to Nany's house one Christmas morning after a big snowstorm. That made a five-year-old girl feel very special." – Joan

"When Dad was at sea, I could hardly wait for him to come home to tell him all the things I did while he was away. Most decisions, even buying new shoes, were put on hold until Dad came home. I loved sports and played on a hockey team for many years but Dad never got the opportunity to come to a game. I never questioned that. It was just part of being a fisherman's son." – Sherman

"Once Dad took me on the *Cape North*. I got seasick and stayed that way throughout the trip that took us about seven miles outside the harbour. The upside was that I got to lie in the captain's bunk. I was with Dad the day he picked up his new car. It was his first car and a rare treat for this seven-year-old, especially when instead of going straight home, he took me for a ride to Bridgewater and drove back to our house by way of Mahone Bay." – Susan

"Since Dad was usually only home for twenty-four-hour periods, I spent as much time as I could around the boat with him. While he got the boat refitted, I often helped his crew fill needles to mend the nets. Growing up I played a lot of sports and Dad always made sure I had good equipment. Although he rarely saw me play, I never questioned his love or support. Maybe it's true the sea gets in your blood, because I too chose to be a fisherman." – David

# Afterword from
# Captain Mitchell

The nine decades of my years have been filled with life and adventure. I would like this book to serve as a vessel to share my experiences with others who love the sea as I do.

I originally told my stories to Ralph Getson, curator at the Fisheries Museum, who reproduced them verbatim as a keepsake for my family and friends. When author Frances Jewel Dickson offered to edit my stories so they could be made available to a broader audience, I was excited at the prospect of sharing my experiences, particularly from my dory fishing days, with as many people as possible.

For those who are not named in this book and whose paths I crossed over the years, I still hold special memories of the events we shared.

The part of my career I spent at the Fisheries Museum provided the opportunity to share some of my stories with thousands of visitors from all over the world. I continue to be blessed with letters, cards and photographs from many of them.

A bounty of gifts has been granted me in the course of my life. My parents, Frederick and Violet, who made my childhood rich with sound values and a healthy fundamental lifestyle. My wife Olive, who bore the lion's share of raising our two daughters and two sons while I was at sea. My children,

Joan, Sherman, Susan and David, who have given me their un-conditional support, particularly since their mother's passing. My grandchildren, Nancy, Debbie, Scott, Tracy, Ian and Lisa, who have always shown an interest in my fishing career. My great-grandchildren Neil, Adam, Emily and Landon; Neil and Adam recently presented school papers based on my career. They all make me proud. As a testimony to their commitment, they surprised their "Pa" with an engraved plate in November 2000. On the same occasion, I received a plaque from Henry Demone, Chief Executive Officer of Highliner Foods, recognizing my contributions to the fishing industry and the Town of Lunenburg, and naming me Honourary Fisherman of the Newfie Days annual celebration. My companion Alice Mills Schwartz, with whom I have shared many happy times and travels in the years since Olive passed away.

My hope is this book will not only provide insights into the bygone days of fishing in schooners for those unfamiliar with that era, but will also bring enjoyment to the reader.

# Acknowledgements

The author gratefully acknowledges Robert Hirtle of Lighthouse Media Group for providing the author photo. The collaborative effort of this work between Captain Matthew Mitchell and the author was greatly facilitated by the many contributions of Ralph Getson, Curator of the Fisheries Museum of the Atlantic in Lunenburg. When we had a question, Ralph had the answer. Photographs and background on the schooners and trawlers Matthew Mitchell served on can be viewed at the Fisheries Museum of the Atlantic.

Some of the details of the earthquake and tsunamis of 1929 were provided by *The History of Burin By Its Senior Citizens*, printed by South Coast Printers Ltd., 1977, Marystown, Newfoundland. Information on compensation received by the victims of these disasters came from *The Tidal Wave* by Garry Cranford, published by Flanker Press Ltd., 2000, St. John's, Newfoundland.

The Newfoundland and Labrador Heritage Web Dictionary of Newfoundland English (www.heritage.nf.ca/dictionary) was most helpful in clarifying expressions used by Captain Mitchell in his Newfoundland vernacular.

Details on the *Young Teazer* were found on the Mahone Bay boat festival website, www.mahonebayclassicboatfestival.org.

## Photo Credits

Thanks to the following for providing photographs:

Matthew Mitchell – pages 17, 97

Judy Allen from the estate of Phyllis Ritcey – pages 16, 25, 26, 28, 29, 36 (top and middle photos), 51

Sherman Creaser from the estate of Owen Creaser – pages 45, 81, 99, 108

Robert Parks – pages 47, 78, 79

Cecil Ritcey – pages 105, 109

Sheila Ritcey – page 36 (bottom photo)

## About the Author

In 1986 Frances Jewel Dickson and her husband Don Zwicker purchased a home along the LaHave River. By happenstance, it proved to be the house where Captain Atwood Parks was born and lived in until he died (1895-1974). Frances's first book was *The DEW Line Years: Voices From the Coldest Cold War*. More information on the author can be found at her website – www.voicesetc.ca.